· WARD LOCK MASTER GARDENER ·

Rock Gardens

JOHN KELLY

WARD LOCK

First published in Great Britain in 1994
by Ward Lock, Villiers House, 41/47 Strand,
London WC2N 5JE, England

A Cassell Imprint

Text © John Kelly 1994
Illustrations © Ward Lock 1994

British Library Cataloguing in Publication Data
is available upon application from The British Library

ISBN 0 7063 7211 5

Text filmset by Litho Link Ltd, Welshpool, Powys
Printed and bound in Singapore by Craft Print Pte Ltd

Previous page: *Saxifraga
cochlearis* 'Minor' growing
on a piece of tufa rock. It is
equally at home planted
in a crevice.

Contents

A properly made rock
garden is a world away from
a mere 'rockery'.

Preface

Long ago, rock gardening consisted of building mini-mountains, sometimes even complete with little roped figures in tweeds, and the more your effort looked like the Matterhorn, so much the better. Later – in the 1920s or thereabouts – the 'rockery' came into vogue. Model mountains were out, but mounds of earth, studded with lumps of rock, were fashionable. Rather as a buttery was a place where butter was sold and a vinery was a greenhouse where vines were grown, so a rockery was essentially a pile of rocks.

With the writings of one or two influential people, notably Reginald Farrer, the 1930s saw the emergence of a more natural approach to the use of rocks in the garden, and the modern era of rock gardening began.

People have always been fascinated by plants, but it was really only in the early years of the twentieth century that plants became generally within the reach of everyone, and not just the rich. Previously, working people had achieved miracles of plant breeding with such things as pinks and auriculas, but choice rock plants changed hands for something like a quarter of a week's wages each. A rock garden was not something a working person could expect to own.

How different it is now! Rock gardening to the very highest standard is open to everyone, even those with practically no garden at all. You can have the most beautiful, small rock garden in a tiny space, inhabited by small plants of ravishing loveliness that, thirty years ago, would have been pronounced too difficult for home gardeners.

A choice alpine now costs, not one quarter of a weekly wage, but about one two-hundredth, and the finest plants are well within the range of us all. Rock is expensive, much more than in days gone by, but we use far less of it now because of our greater understanding of *how* to use it.

In this book, the term 'rockery' has been left out completely. We are not in the business of breeding rocks, but of using them in the most natural manner possible to make a home-from-home for the plants of the high mountains.

However, there are still many people who think of a rock garden as a 'rockery'. They will, on finding themselves with a pile of earth left over from levelling work or making a pond, push bits of stone into it and plant it with *Cerastium tomentosum* (snow-in-summer). There is nothing to be ashamed of in this, as we all have to start somewhere, but I hope to persuade you that by tackling things another way you can begin to enjoy what is, when all is said and done, one of the most fascinating forms of gardening there is.

If you are considering the 'fish pond and rockery' option, read this book before you go ahead and see whether you would not rather go down a more interesting gardening route. If you already have a rock garden or are reasonably well versed in the art of rock gardening, stay with me. You may still learn something new. J.K.

ACKNOWLEDGEMENTS

The publishers would like to thank the following for
supplying photographs for this book: A–Z Botanical
Collection: p. 61; Pat Brindley: pp. 80 (bottom), 72 (top):
Garden Picture Library: pp. 4, 9, 12, 16, 28, 37, 44, 48,
49, 65, 84; Jerry Harpur: pp. 64, 81; Clive Nichols: pp. 8,
25, 33, 52, 56, 57 (bottom), 60, 69, 73, 85, 89, 92, 93;
Hugh Palmer: p. 41; Photos Horticultural: pp. 13, 21,
24; Wildlife Matters: pp. 29, 32.

The line illustrations were drawn by David Woodroffe
and Jonathan Adams.

· 1 ·
Where to
Build a Rock Garden

The question to answer first is really *why* you want to build a rock garden. The chances are that the reason will be one of these:

1. Your first interest is in having a water feature and you think a rock garden would be its natural companion.

2. You think a rock garden would, in a general way, improve the look of the garden as a whole.

3. The layout, aspect, slope and other factors strongly suggest that a rock garden would fit in naturally.

4. Your garden is small, and a rock garden would let you grow many more plants because rock plants, too, are small.

5. A rocky feature would provide a textural change from soil, paths and lawns.

6. You would love to grow alpine and rock plants because they just happen to appeal to you.

Any one or combination of these reasons provides complete justification for you to start planning immediately. The next step is to work out just where your rock garden should be.

The short history of rock gardening in the preface of this book showed how rock gardens changed over the decades from being primarily mounds decorated with rock to becoming principally tailor-made homes for mountain-dwelling plants.

It does not matter what your reason is for wanting to create a rock garden; your choice of site must put the plants first. If you choose a position the plants do not like, you will end up with rock and not much else, and be back to the old style 'rockery' that we want so much to avoid.

This means, for example, that if you want to make a water feature with a rock garden attached, you should think of the needs of the plants first, even if it means putting the pond somewhere other than in the position you first thought of.

Once you have taken all the factors that affect the plants into consideration, you can then bear them in mind while you turn to the question of the general garden design and how the rock garden can be made best to fit into it.

FACTORS AFFECTING PLANTS

In order to have healthy, long-lived compact rock plants that will grow well and flower generously, several factors must suit them. These are soil, light, moisture, climate and exposure.

Soil

The most important thing of all to remember is that no matter what type of garden soil you have, it can be improved to make it suitable as a rock garden soil. However, there are two main kinds of soil – alkaline and acid – that greatly influence the kinds of plants that you can grow.

● *Alkaline soils* usually contain 'lime' in some form or other, although in parts of Australia and North America alkalinity is caused by caustic compounds. Limy soils will grow a very wide range of plants, whereas caustic soils are more limiting.

On the whole, it is not worth trying to convert a limy soil to an acid one, as it is highly unlikely that you will be able to do this successfully. For specialized rock garden environments, which we will look at later, it is possible to create situations in which imported, acid soil is kept separate from the general garden soil, but for the main rock garden it is best to accept your limy soil as it is and avoid trying to grow plants such as dwarf rhododendrons, gaultherias and asiatic gentians.

● *Acid soils* There is no point in liming acid soils. Very few indeed are too acid for the majority of rock plants and, despite what used to be thought, there are hardly any plants that *must* have lime.

● *Heavy and light soils* can each be improved by the liberal addition of organic matter. Peat is an excellent soil conditioner, but if you think you should not be using peat for environmental reasons, you can use something else. The cheapest method, and one that will provide the greatest bulk of organic matter, is to buy a dozen bales of straw and stack them in the open. They will rot down in a year or so to a lovely, friable compost that will greatly improve the most unfriendly soil.

Good drainage is absolutely vital. Alpine and rock plants just will not grow if the soil is waterlogged, stagnant and sour. In practice, however, drainage is rarely a problem, as rock gardens tend to be built up above the general level of the garden. Nevertheless, you should bear it in mind and make sure that the site drains freely. At the very least, you do not want the

◀ While the quality of the soil is important, it is only the provision of good drainage that will allow a high population of thriving rock plants such as this sedum and creeping Jenny (*Lysimachia nummularia*).

When a rock garden is skilfully made on a flat site, the flatness tends to be much less noticeable.

ground round the edges of the rock garden churned to mud every time you do some planting or weeding.

Light

There is not much we can do about the natural light levels, but it is interesting to note the large variations even within the same country. The difference of just a few hundred miles could mean that in one area the light levels are such that plants like the cushion saxifrages would need to be shaded at mid-day whilst in another they do not.

As a specific example, Edinburgh, Scotland, is on the latitude of Schefferville, Labrador, and the southern part of Hudson's Bay, New York, on the other hand, is roughly level with Rome and

Fig. 1 The worst place for a rock garden is under or close to a tree.

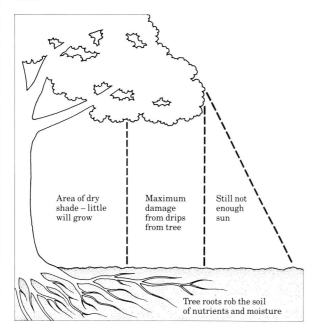

Madrid. Plants that may well benefit from part shade in New York are quite likely to flower poorly if given the same treatment in Edinburgh.

So you should bear such factors in mind in the face of the best general advice, which is to build your rock garden in a sunny place and use its structure to provide shady pockets and a shady side. If you are really keen on having part of the rock garden in some shade, the best plan is to arrange it so that the dappled shade of trees falls on it. But you must never position the rock garden or part of it directly under trees, as any plants subject to rain dripping from the foliage will be killed (Fig. 1).

Moisture

Water is a major factor in rock gardening. We have already looked at drainage, which is a problem of the disposal of moisture. By improving your soil by the addition of generous amounts of organic matter, you will have made it more moisture retentive. However, you should still consider watering to be an essential operation, especially with newly planted plants. Rock gardens and their plants do not take kindly to sprinkler watering, and you should be prepared to water by hand. With this in mind, make sure that you do not build your rock garden where watering will be difficult.

Climate and exposure

While you cannot influence the climate of the area in which you live, you can profoundly change its impact on your garden in general and your rock garden in particular.

Firstly, though, you should be aware of the hardiness of plants. This usually refers to cold resistance, but in Australia hardiness has to do with a plant's ability to tolerate heat. Most alpines and rock plants are highly cold-tolerant, so gardeners in Britain, most of New Zealand and the northern parts of North America will have few problems. Australian gardeners may have to be more selective.

For the open rock garden, you should avoid all plants whose descriptions in books or nursery catalogues include such phrases as 'may benefit from some protection from winter damp'. What this usually means is that the plants have woolly leaves and will almost certainly die if asked to grow outside where the winters are wet.

On the other hand, if you experience prolonged snowfall as part of your regular climate, such plants will feel completely at home and will be dry, warm and cosy under their insulating blanket.

In general, rock plants are wind resistant. (Their natural habitat is one in which wind is seldom absent). However, some plants that are not quite as hardy as others will benefit from being sheltered from wind, so if you can site the rock garden downwind of a hedge or a group of shrubs, but not in the shade of either, and not so close that the soil will be robbed by them, so much the better.

Walls and solid fences provide much less shelter than you might think and in fact can cause damaging swirls and accelerations of wind. On the other hand, permeable structures such as hedges filter the wind and provide good shelter for a distance downwind equivalent to about six times their height.

FACTORS AFFECTING DESIGN

Once you have taken the needs of the plants into consideration, bear them constantly in mind while you look at the garden with a view to deciding where to site the rock garden. You will now be looking at such questions as whether to make the rock garden in the lawn, beside a path, on the flat or on a slope, and so on.

Where not to build

Never make a rock garden in the most neglected corner of the garden. All too often, people design their gardens beautifully, only to find that they have an odd space that they have either overlooked or preferred to ignore for some reason – poor soil, bad drainage, poor light or whatever. They ponder for a while and then come up with the answer, 'I know, let's make it into a rock garden'.

This is the worst possible way to start what should be a most absorbing and delightful form of gardening. If it is at all possible, the rock garden should be given the best, not the worst position in the whole garden. Think positively!

Size

A great many rock gardens are built on lawns, usually after the family has grown past the age when the maximum amount of grass is required. However, the principles of building are exactly the same whether or not the lawn is robbed for the space, and the main one is to build big enough.

It is most important that you should be able to see the finished article in your mind's eye. It is a major mistake to plan your rock garden on too small a scale. If it is completely detached from the borders and is in fact an island site, it will look plain silly if it is too small.

There are two kinds of rock garden one sees that have been made too small. One is the thin, wavy sort, not much more than 45 cm (18 in) wide, with no real structure at all and a perfect nuisance when you want to mow round it. The other is the classic rock bun, sitting all on its own like an abandoned sand castle.

◄ Saxifrages and small
pinks in a rock garden built
on a slope.

▲ The lawn remains
undamaged by foot traffic
when a sympathetically
designed path borders the
rock garden.

13

If you are going to build a rock garden, plan for it to be as large as you dare, and then if possible allow for it to be a little larger. You will certainly not regret it.

Avoiding damage during building

It is not good policy to think of cutting a rock garden out of the lawn and planning to run the lawn right up to it, or with a narrow gap between

Fig. 2 Laying a path round the rock garden before you begin constructing the rock garden itself.

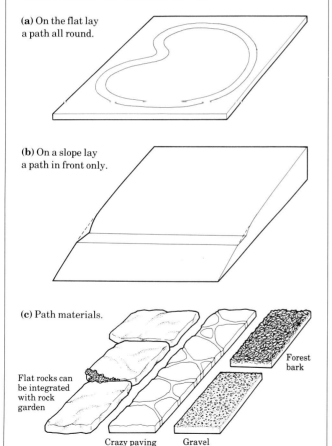

(a) On the flat lay a path all round.

(b) On a slope lay a path in front only.

(c) Path materials.

Flat rocks can be integrated with rock garden

Forest bark

Crazy paving   Gravel

the grass and the stones. This applies whether the rock garden is surrounded by lawn or just cut out from one side. The reason is that there will be a lot of foot traffic around the rock garden. Planting, weeding and even just admiring will soon make an unsightly mess of a strip of land 60 cm (24 in) wide.

The building operation will damage the immediate surroundings. The compaction of the soil alone will be enough to do lasting damage. This factor is important when building a rock garden anywhere.

The way to avoid these troubles is to make a path round the rock garden before you do anything else (Fig. 2). It can be either a distinct and apparently deliberate path, or it can be a series of large, flat stones made to be an integral part of the rock garden and in the same rock that you will be using for the rock garden itself. The type of stone you choose will depend on what stone is available, how the price works out, and your own personal design preference.

On the flat or on a slope?

So far, you will have decided on the best position for your rock garden. You know that you want to build it in sun, with perhaps a little dappled shade, that you want to make it big enough to be a real feature, and that you will make sure the traffic round its boundaries will cause no damage.

On this last point, there is an exception to the need to provide all-round protection against wear. This is the outcrop garden on a slope. Here, the main area of probable wear is immediately in front; the rest is not nearly as vulnerable. It will, in fact, only look really natural if, when made in a lawn, the grass comes quite closely up to the rocks at the top and sides. You will find it much easier to work on an outcrop by standing on the stones themselves than on the sloping ground.

Rock gardens look at their most natural when built on slopes. They help, too, to stabilize steep slopes and to prevent the run-off of soil caused by rain. If you have the space you can build several outcrops, which together make up one quite large rock garden separated by grass or larger plants, such as shrubs and perennials. Sloping outcrop rock gardens are easier and more economical to build than those on the flat.

If you build your rock garden on the flat, the main thing to have in mind is that it should look as though it is a natural part of the landscape – that it has been there perhaps for hundreds of years before your house was even thought of. It should appear to be just the tip of a large, underground rock system that happened to break the surface in precisely that spot. The last thing you want is for it to look artificial and out of place.

The rock garden as part of the border
The rock garden can be part of the ordinary border and still look perfectly natural. In nature the rocks have to end somewhere, and they often merge into pebbly scree, which itself gradually becomes more and more loamy and eventually grades into land that supports tall flowers and grasses.

You can make this kind of rock garden at the back or front of the border, somewhere along its length, or at its end. You can take up the whole depth of the border, with the heights of the taller plants balanced more by rock than by rock plants, although its general profile will be lower.

Small spaces
Although this book is about rock gardening, it is also about growing rock plants in places that have all the attributes of their natural homes. These may be completely different from the conventional rock garden but will almost always be stony, if not rocky. As well as in rock gardens, you can grow rock plants in:

● *Raised beds* These can be of any height, from about 30 cm (12 in) to 1.2 m (4 ft), but are usually

---

· PLANTS FOR GROWING IN PAVING ·

It is best to start off with seeds sown in the cracks of the paving or by planting small seedlings and taking good care of them for some weeks.

Name	Description
Anacyclus depressus	Grey leaves, white daisies.
Armeria caespitosa	A tiny 'thrift'.
Campanula cochleariifolia	Dainty, blue, hanging bells.
Campanula garganica	Masses of starry blue on low mats.
Dianthus (pinks) – the dwarf species and hybrids	Mat-forming in various shades of pink.
Dryas octopetala (mountain avens)	Oak-leaved mats.
Erinus alpinus	White, pink or red, small 'spot' plants.
Erodium (storksbills) – the dwarfer species	Small mat of neat leaves; stemless flowers.
Mentha requinii	A tiny, creeping mint, aromatic.
Phlox douglasii	Neat mats in many colours.
Sempervivum (house leeks) – the smaller types	Attractive, fleshy rosettes.
Thymus – many kinds, including the lemon thymes	Mat-forming with minute leaves.
Veronica prostrata	A small, ground-hugging speedwell.

Making the best of a steep bank by growing rock plants. Even more could have been made of it if provision had been made for planting in the retaining wall.

about 75 cm (30 in) high. They enable tiny, choice plants to be grown closer to the eye, the gardener has closer control over soil conditions, and they are ideal for disabled gardeners.

● *Troughs and sinks* Nowadays, these are more likely to be artificially made than of real stone, but they can be made to look very realistic. If you have hardly any garden at all, a few of these will allow you to grow a surprising number of plants.

● *Screes* A scree (see pages 45–47) is a deep, stony feature that can appear on its own in the most formal or smallest of gardens. It can also be incorporated as part of a rock garden.

● *Walls* Wherever you can build a retaining wall – a very steep bank, or alongside steps, for example – you can grow rock plants, especially those that revel in being grown on their sides.

All these are variations on the rock garden. You can create rocky homes for plants in a raised bed or even a sink garden. As long as you avoid dank, dark, over-shadowed corners, you can enjoy rock gardening anywhere.

· 2 ·
Introducing Rock Plants

Most people are unclear about the differences, if any, between a rock plant and an alpine. This is not surprising, as there is no very sharp distinction in practice. In theory there is rather more.

A rock plant is one whose natural habitat is a rocky one. Botanists will tell you that an alpine is a plant which grows between the permanent tree line and the permanent snow line, and will use words like 'sub-alpine'. Quite honestly, such concerns matter little to gardeners, for whom a rock plant can be said to be any plant that looks right in a rock garden.

Of course, tastes vary greatly and can be extreme. Nevertheless, if someone wishes to grow giant sunflowers on his rock garden, who are we to tell him not to? Your garden is your domain, in which, if nowhere else, you should be allowed full rein to your self expression, as long as the neighbours do not mind.

On the other hand, it should be acknowledged that there is a general consensus about which plants are appropriate for the rock garden. It is impossible to sum it up in a sentence or a snappy definition, but it should become clear by the end of this chapter.

Characteristics of rock plants
Rock plants and alpines vary enormously, from tiny, hard cushions to small shrubs. Their flower stems may be entirely absent or up to 60 cm (24 in) high, depending on which ones you allow in to the category, as it were. Nevertheless, all have certain definite tendencies in common:

1. They tend to have flowers that are large for the sizes of the plants, usually because of reduction in stem height.

2. Many have their foliage reduced to tight cushions or low mats.

3. They tend to be happy when permitted to send their roots on long, deep quests for moisture.

4. They are usually vulnerable to wet lodging round their necks and do not take kindly to soil being splashed onto their leaves.

5. They are adapted to resist wind, and thus remain short and tough and do not need to be staked.

6. Most – but by no means all – have short flowering seasons because the growing season in the mountains is so short.

What these points mean in practical terms is that you have plants that are generally small, compact and usually quite dramatically full of flower, and that the best way to enjoy them is to grow as many as you can and choose them so that there are flowers on your rock garden for as much of the year as possible.

They must also be provided with excellent drainage and should be top-dressed with gravel in order to keep their necks free of damp and their leaves free of soil splash.

Mat-forming plants (Fig. 3)
A very large number of rock plants are ground-hugging and grow as mats of branches and foliage. Many are technically shrubs or sub-shrubs (plants whose tops are part woody and part soft) and there are far fewer herbaceous plants, dying away for winter, than you might think. In fact, the proportion of evergreens is a good deal higher than among garden plants as a whole. This is largely because they have evolved to spend their winters under a protective, dry blanket of snow in a dormant state. It is worth repeating again that, although they are adapted to resisting wind, the freezing winds of a lowland winter, combined with an absence of snow cover and generally wet conditions, can readily be lethal to them, and it is for these reasons that shelter from wind is a great help, as is the provision of ways of reducing the effects of wetness.

● *Sites for mat-forming plants* Mat-formers usually give of their best if they are encouraged to tumble over rocks and often if planted in crevices between them. Aubrietas, for example, always look at their best when growing nearly vertically. These lovely, well-known plants are easy enough to grow, but if you allow wetness to accumulate on their branches when they are growing on the flat, they will tend to become patchy and straggly, instead of full and firm.

The mat-forming plants are the mainstay of the rock garden. It is they that give the masses of colour and form the carpeting element, and you should choose them with care, bearing in mind the colour succession. Among the main groups are: aubrietas (early to late spring), phloxes (mid-spring to early summer), thymes (mid-spring to mid-summer), rock garden pinks (early to late summer), helianthemums (early to late summer) – these are really prostrate shrubs – and cam-

---

· CREVICE-LOVING PLANTS ·

Name	Description
Aethionema 'Warley Rose'	Small and bushy with rose-pink flowers in late spring.
Androsace lanuginosa	Trailing, woolly leaves, pink flowers in spring.
Campanula 'Haylodgensis'	Double powder blue flowers in summer.
Genista humifusa	Tiny broom, yellow flowers in early summer.
Geranium 'Ballerina'	Mauve flowers veined purple in summer.
Helichrysum milfordiae	White everlastings on woolly-silky, grey cushions; suitable for a rock overhang.
Vitaliana primuliflora	Grey cushions with yellow flowers in spring.
Lewisia hybrids	Bright flowers in summer; grow on its side.
Moltkia intermedia	Shrublet with bright blue summer flowers.
Phlox douglasii varieties	Neat cushions, many colours.
Phyteuma comosum	Clusters of bottle-shaped flowers in summer; tricky on the flat: quite easy in a crevice.
Primula species – many of the European kinds	Attractive flowers in mid to late spring.
Ramonda myconi	Purple 'potato' flowers over green rosettes in summer; for shade.
Saxifraga species – all except the 'mossy' saxifrages	Grey-green or silver cushions; various colour flowers in summer.
Sedum – all types	Neat mounds of soft, fleshy leaves; summer flowers in yellow, pink and white.
Sempervivum species (house leeks) – all types	Attractive, fleshy leaves.

panulas (early summer to early autumn) – which are mostly herbaceous.

There are many, many more mat-forming rock plants, but these major groups form the backbone of the rock garden planting.

Crevice-loving plants (Fig. 3)

Although mat-formers can be grown just about anywhere on the rock garden, and many of them enjoy being planted in crevices, there is another class of rock plants altogether, consisting of those that are true crevice-lovers. These are plants that in nature grow, not on screes or rocky debris, but on rock faces that are riven by fissures. They are adapted to this kind of habitat and respond well if you can repeat it in the garden.

● *Adaptations* One way in which crevice-loving plants are adapted to their habitat is very important when it comes to the 'rightness' of the appearance of the plants. Crevice plants with long flowering stems, such as the silver saxifrages, look better when the sprays emerge near the horizontal and arch gracefully together than when planted on the flat, in which case their flowering stems splay out at all sorts of angles.

The crevices provide shelter, too, from driving rain and battering winds. This is especially important in the wild, and while your garden is not as harsh an environment as a high mountain, a plant adapted to such conditions may not thrive when fully exposed to the elements.

Other plants, such as the beautiful lewisias from North America, must never have water lying on their leaves or around their necks. Lewisias are thought of as difficult plants, but are not really, as they can live happily for years if given tight, vertical crevices in which to grow.

The same applies to the shade-loving ramondas, which make round, dark green, cabbagey rosettes on the surfaces of the rocks if their necks are in crevices. If they were on the flat, they would soon rot.

Crevices also provide cool, moist root runs for plants used to driving their roots deeply in search of constant moisture. Use the crevices between the rocks as well as the soil pockets, and you are likely to have far fewer problems with drought and watering.

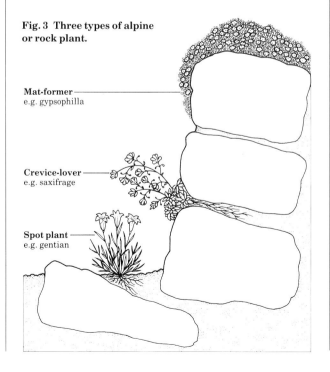

Fig. 3 Three types of alpine or rock plant.

Mat-former
e.g. gypsophilla

Crevice-lover
e.g. saxifrage

Spot plant
e.g. gentian

▲ *Phlox* 'Chattahoochee' is an example of a larger, more open kind of mat-forming plant. On a small rock garden it is tall enough to be a spot plant.

◄ *Lewisia* 'Pinkie' – a plant that must be grown on its side and is ideal for a crevice.

Primula polyneura – an
attractive spot plant
growing in a small rock
garden made from tufa rock.

Spot plants (Fig. 3)

Your main rock garden planting will consist of mat-forming plants and crevice dwellers, but what will give it its distinctive character will be the plants that serve as accents.

A rock garden planted exclusively with plants that form mats would be dull, even if brightly coloured, as everything would be flat with few vertical accents. Adding crevice lovers does not

· SPOT PLANTS ·

Name	Description
Alliums (ornamental onions) – all types	Large, rounded heads of rich red in early summer.
Anemone blanda	Blue, red, white; mid spring.
Aquilegias	All types flower in late spring or early summer.
Betula nana	A dwarf birch, only 30 cm (1 ft) high.
Celmisias	Several species of silvery-leafed, upright plants with large, white daisies.
Crocuses	Many species, flowering in spring, autumn and winter.
Cyclamen	Dwarf species, flowering in every season.
Daphnes	Several small shrubs, flowering in spring and early summer.
Dianthus	Some rock garden pinks are spot plants, while others are mat-formers.
Dodecatheon	Taller plants for shady places; flower in summer.
Euryops acraeus	Silver 'bun' with golden daisies in summer.
Hypericum olympicum	Large, yellow flowers in summer.
Irises	Many small irises flower in spring and summer.
Narcissus – dwarf species and varieties	Several types under 25 cm (10 in) high. Good spot plants.
Primulas	Good spot plants.
Rhododendrons	There are many neat, dwarf kinds.

change this much, and the rock garden needs upright plants to give it balance. By the same token, too many erect plants make a rock garden look untidy and unnatural. Furthermore, once you start adding plants that are too tall, the whole balance is ruined and the right effect is lost. On the whole, the vertical component of the average-sized rock garden should consist of plants whose maximum height in flower is not more than 30 cm (12 in).

Dwarf trees, dwarf conifers (Fig. 4)

The only plants to exceed around 30 cm (12 in) should be dwarf trees, including dwarf conifers. Conifers on a rock garden must be really dwarf, not merely slow growing, otherwise they will soon become far too large. You must expect a dwarf conifer to be really small when you buy it; don't be tempted by false bargains.

The right sort of conifer will not grow to much more than 1.2 m (4 ft) in 30 years. This may sound incredibly slow, but if you imagine one that size and with about that spread of branches on your rock garden, you have to admit that anything larger would be entirely out of proportion. If, when you buy it, it is only about 8 cm (3 in) tall, that should be perfectly reasonable.

Foliage

Conifers are, of course, grown for their foliage, and you should pay quite close attention to the foliage component of the rock garden. Some people become too obsessive about it, but it is still true that flowers are with us for a short time, whereas foliage is much more of a long-term feature. On the rock garden, where so many plants are evergreen, it is even more so.

The rock garden is not the place for large-leaved plants which would not survive a mountain environment, but quietly beautiful effects result when you bear in mind the effects of the small but significant leaves of such spot plants as dwarf-bearded irises, sisyrinchiums, primulas and aquilegias among the carpets of phlox and aubrieta.

Spread of plants

Just as much as height, you should take spread into consideration. Those whose profession is selling plants know that the most common question asked by people buying rock plants is, 'will it spread?'. The trouble is that they want to know for the wrong reason: they are looking for fast results.

Cerastium tomentosum (snow-in-summer) will spread all right – in fact it will take over everything – and is the last sort of plant you want. On the other hand, you may not be ready at this stage to plant the ultimate sorts of rarities that hardly spread at all. You need to know roughly to what extent a given plant will spread after, say, three and five years – so ask.

There is nothing worse than seeing your nice spot plants overwhelmed by mat-forming ones or worrying about how to extricate a choice crevice dweller from an incoming tide of iberis or *Phlox subulata*. It helps to know, for example, that this phlox is likely to spread twice as far and fast as a variety of *Phlox douglasii*. The A–Z of Plants at the end of this book will help, but never be afraid to ask an expert.

Fig. 4 Comparative heights of some widely grown 'dwarf' conifers after 25 years.

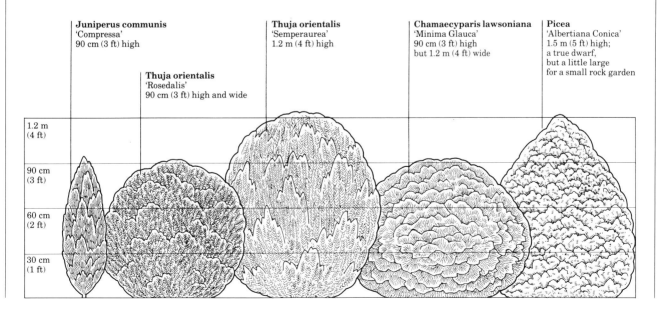

Juniperus communis 'Compressa' 90 cm (3 ft) high

Thuja orientalis 'Rosedalis' 90 cm (3 ft) high and wide

Thuja orientalis 'Semperaurea' 1.2 m (4 ft) high

Chamaecyparis lawsoniana 'Minima Glauca' 90 cm (3 ft) high but 1.2 m (4 ft) wide

Picea 'Albertiana Conica' 1.5 m (5 ft) high; a true dwarf, but a little large for a small rock garden

1.2 m (4 ft)

90 cm (3 ft)

60 cm (2 ft)

30 cm (1 ft)

Bulbs

The same general rule about what looks right applies to bulbs as it does to other plants. Many a rock garden has been spoilt after being thoughtfully planted with above-ground plants and then carelessly scattered with big daffodils and tulips.

Size is one factor; naturalness of appearance is another. The 45 cm (18 in) daffodil 'King Alfred' is not appropriate but 'Tête à Tête', which is less than 20 cm (8 in), is ideal. Similarly, Darwin tulips look dreadful on a rock garden, whereas the species tulips and dwarf hybrids are perfect. You would not plant big, fat Dutch crocuses, but the much daintier, easy-to-grow varieties of *C. chrysanthus*, of which there are about 30, make a fine show in spring and are perfectly in proportion.

Dwarf shrubs

Many rock plants are, in fact, shrubs. We have a tendency to want to categorize plants into 'types' and put them neatly into pigeon holes – shrubs, bulbs, perennials, rock plants, for example — but this carries with it certain dangers.

One of these is that we tend to accept the entire pigeon hole, rather than sorting out a few items from it. Just as with bulbs, you should choose only the dwarfer ones and those that look most natural (not show narcissi, for instance), so with shrubs you should plant only those that are aesthetically suited to the rock garden.

This may sound strange, but when it comes to shrubs for the rock garden is where many gardeners go wrong. Mention 'shrubs' and they look in the mental pigeon hole where deutzias, philadelphus and lilacs live. Rock garden shrubs are sometimes related to regular garden shrubs (as, for example, dwarf rhododendrons are), but not often.

For example, the vast range of cotoneasters only includes about two that are suitable for the

◄ **Dwarf shrubs and conifers provide a firmness of design that complements the strength of the rock features.**

▲ **Some smaller daffodils growing in close company with *Helleborus foetidus*.**

smaller rock garden, while *Berberis* rates only one. *Penstemon*, however, which most people have in the 'perennials' pigeon hole, is a source of several first-class rock garden shrubs. *Gaultheria*, a genus of shrubs related to rhododendrons, furnishes just one rather coarse shrub for the garden at large, whereas for peaty, shaded places on the rock garden it provides us with more than a dozen species.

Dwarf shrubs, because of their permanent, woody branch structure, join dwarf trees (of which there are very few) and dwarf conifers in forming the architectural element of the planting, and these, with the rocks, will determine the year-round character of your rock garden.

Succession of flowering

A great many people think that rock gardens are purely spring features, and this general idea has the effect of making more and more gardeners create spring rock gardens. This is not entirely helped by garden centre managers who, perfectly understandably, stock up to meet the demand.

The rock garden can and should have flowers in it during every month of the year. Even in the dark, cold months of winter there are tough, hardy bulbs and plants such as the tiny *Cyclamen coum* that are perfect for cheering up a gloomy day. If you have never seen the little *Iris reticulata* flowering through the snow in late winter or marvelled at the toughness of *Crocus imperati* in late autumn, when nothing much else is happening in the world of flowers, you have missed part of what rock gardening is all about (Fig. 5).

The big mistake people often make with a new rock garden is to buy all the plants at one go and, while doing so, to fall for the ones in flower. It is worth taking much more trouble than that.

The names of rock plants

As you will already have seen, it is impossible to discuss alpines and rock plants without using Latin names. Most people would love it if all plants had 'common' names. Unfortunately, you find different 'common' names for the same plant among English speakers. Wake Robin, for example, is an arum in England, but a trillium in America.

In this book you will find common names used as much as possible, but don't forget that true common names are very old, and the English language is not traditional in the European Alps, the Caucasus or the Himalayas, where most of the plants come from. Botanical Latin names are not nearly as difficult as you may think. After all, we use delphinium, chrysanthemum, rhododendron and antirrhinum as common names without turning a hair, so why not *Dianthus* and *Saxifraga*?

Plants are listed in books under the Latin names, so it helps to use them when looking for further information. Information, too, can be gained from the name themselves. The word *palustris* after the name of the genus (the first name), for example, means 'of the marsh', so you would not put such a plant in the hottest, driest part of the rock garden. The same thing applies to *sylvestris*, which means 'of the woods'.

Of course there are aubrietas, phloxes, crocuses, campanulas, primulas and penstemons, but these familiar names are all Latin. Many more will be just as friendly to you before long.

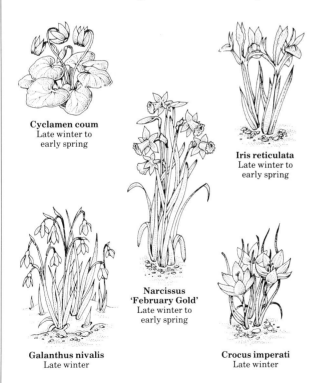

Cyclamen coum
Late winter to early spring

Iris reticulata
Late winter to early spring

Narcissus 'February Gold'
Late winter to early spring

Galanthus nivalis
Late winter

Crocus imperati
Late winter

Fig. 5 Bulbs for late winter and early spring.

· 3 ·
How to
Build a Rock Garden

There is probably no other type of gardening – outdoors at any rate – that involves you so completely in the home comforts of plants as making a rock garden. As long as you constantly bear in mind that the plants come first, and you are making a rock garden and not a rockery, you will find the actual building to be one of the most enjoyable garden projects you have ever undertaken.

When to build

The best time of year to build a rock garden is in the summer. There is nothing worse than having to contend with a wet spring, when the soil is still not warm enough to dry up quickly. The alternative, especially for those who live in areas where summers are hot, is to build the rock garden in the early autumn.

You cannot build a rock garden when the soil is wet and cold. The result will be compacted and airless. Choosing a time when the odd shower will make little difference is both more comfortable for you and infinitely better for the plants.

Preparation

As you have already decided where the rock garden is to be and have mapped out its outline, even to the extent of laying a path round it so that

the work will not ruin the surrounding soil, the next step is to prepare the soil of the rock garden itself.

1. If you are taking the area from the lawn, cut the sods square and a full spit deep. Turn each on its side and, with one foot on it, slice the top 2–5 cm (1–2 in) off with the spade. These turves make excellent loam if you stack them neatly, upside down against a wall.

2. If you are building on ordinary garden soil, double-dig the site. After you have dug your first spit, break up the soil beneath it to the depth of another spit. This greatly assists drainage.

3. Now break up any remaining clods of soil and work them down until they can be mixed with the organic matter you are providing, which should bulk up the soil by up to one third of its volume. (Sand, which is often recommended, is not necessary and leads to the creation of a fast-drying soil. It is the organic matter that lightens a heavy soil.)

4. Add fine gravel to the mixture to bulk it up once more, this time by about one fifth.

When you have carried out these operations, you should find yourself with quite a substantial mound of soil. It is a mistake to try to make this

into the shape you want the rock garden to be (apart from its outline). The rocks will to a very large extent dictate how the rock garden will shape up. You should have a general idea to work to, but be prepared to be flexible in your ideas.

Choosing the rock

There are many kinds of rocks from which you can choose for rock-garden making, but on the whole you will be restricted by what is available locally and by price. The following is a rough guide to the major kinds of rocks.

● *Quartz* This is sometimes sold as 'rockery stone' and should be avoided. It is bone-white, with a crystalline appearance, and comes in shapeless lumps with no faces. It is unsympathetic to plants.

● *Granite* This dense rock can be used to make attractive rock gardens, but it is very difficult to manage anything other than smallish pieces. It is angular and forbidding in appearance, although faces can usually be discerned.

● *Gritstones* These hard rocks are dense and not very easy to work with. However, they are capable of weathering attractively and are not inimical to plants.

● *Limestone* There are many kinds of limestone. The softest (called chalk in the U.K., but almost absent in North America and Australia) are unsuitable, but harder limestones make ideal rock garden stone. They weather beautifully and usually have well-defined faces. Limestone pavement (not a road surface, but a natural, fractured landscape feature) is an environmental treasure and should never be available to rock gardeners.

◀ **Well-chosen rock, cleverly natural water pouring over slate, and a contented population of plants.**

▲ **Water-worn limestone. You should be very careful that you do not encourage the taking of surface limestone from environmentally important sites.**

Fig 6. Moving heavy rocks.

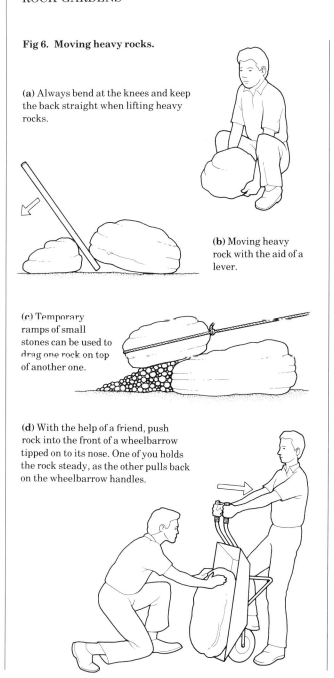

(a) Always bend at the knees and keep the back straight when lifting heavy rocks.

(b) Moving heavy rock with the aid of a lever.

(c) Temporary ramps of small stones can be used to drag one rock on top of another one.

(d) With the help of a friend, push rock into the front of a wheelbarrow tipped on to its nose. One of you holds the rock steady, as the other pulls back on the wheelbarrow handles.

● *Sandstones* Sandstones comprise the best general group of rocks. There are a great many kinds, from almost black to light ochre-yellow and russet-red, and almost all of them are attractive, easy to work, not too heavy, and well suited to plants.

● *Schists, micas, etc.* Any of the rocks that are made up of packed layers are unsuitable, as they will split under the action of heat and frost. They may be cheap to obtain and are often light, but apart from their structure, they may also contain oils or other chemicals that are generally bad for plants.

Rock is seldom cheap, unless you have a source outside the market. However, you are creating a feature every bit as attractive and important to your garden as a greenhouse or a gazebo, so the expense will be worthwhile.

You must try not to become miserly with the rocks. To build a proper rock garden, much of the rock on which you have spent good money will have to be buried. If you try to arrange things so that you can see where your money went, you will end up with something like an almond pudding or a dog's graveyard – the two classic calamities of rock garden construction.

The effect to aim for

The reason why you will bury much of the rock is bound up with producing a natural effect. In fact you do not completely bury any single rock; it is the proportion of each one that is above or below ground that matters.

The essential effect to aim for is to make your rock garden appear as though it were an outcrop of rock that existed on the site on which your home was built, and which you have managed, with great skill and knowledge of plants, to turn into an essential and integral part of your garden.

You will not achieve this if the rocks merely sit on the surface, neither will you do so if each rock does not relate naturally to its neighbour.

If you take a trip to the country and look at rocks, you will see that they are always arranged in strata (layers), usually running across your field of vision, either horizontally or at an angle. The strata are also split vertically or at an angle to the vertical. The effect is as if the cliff, bluff or outcrop at which you are looking was made up of blocks whose shapes are irregular but whose overall effect when combined is of a sort of rough regularity (Fig. 7).

What you see of each rock is mostly one face, as the rest is hidden within the outcrop. Some rocks will present their entire outer faces, while others will show only parts of them. If you set out to show as much of each rock as possible, including all its faces, you will end up with something like the monoliths of Easter Island, not a natural rock outcrop. The latter is what you should aim for, if not to reproduce, then to achieve approximately and, of course, on a scale that is appropriate to the size of your garden and also the site of the rock garden.

The first layer of rocks
Start laying rocks somewhere at the edge, or just inside the line of the path you have made. The first rock is important; get this one right and you are likely to build a good rock garden. Don't try to rush it. Tempo is as necessary to rock-garden building as it is to the game of golf.

Don't set the rock on the soil; set it into the soil by about one third of its height and at a backward-sloping angle. The purpose of this is two-fold and it applies to all the rocks.

1. By setting the rocks into the soil and not on it, you set up the sort of firm structure that will allow you to walk on the rocks without their rocking by as much as a millimetre.

2. By setting them with a backwards slant, you encourage rain to run backwards into the soil of the rock garden. With a forward or level tilt, you would lose much of the precious rain. It is obvious that this factor is most important with the first layer.

It is the first layer that determines the outline shape of the rock garden, but it is not a good idea to lay it all at once. Lay in a few rocks, and then start on the second layer (see page 34). Doing it this way is less boring and it allows you greater flexibility as you build.

Fig. 7 Laying rocks so that they appear natural.

(a) Correct: strata follows the same slanting plane with approximately one-third of the rock buried.

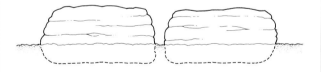

(b) Correct: strata follows the same horizontal plane with approximately one-third of the rock buried.

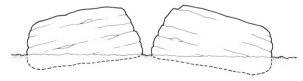

(c) Incorrect: strata is at different angles and not enough of the rock is buried.

The method of laying rocks (Fig. 8)

Before you lay each rock and after you have dug out its bed, cover the bed with soil as nearly to the shape of the under surface of the rock as possible. This will go a long way to preventing the occurrence of air pockets. Air pockets under, beside and between the rocks are a major cause of recurring problems. Mice, slugs, snails, woodlice and ants will all make use of them as redoubts from which to mount highly successful attacks on your plants. To prevent this, you should ram the soil under each rock and particularly behind it. Ramming at the sides comes after the next rocks to the first having been placed.

Ramming means just that – plenty of force. I use my hand, almost karate-style, with the force delivered by the tips of stiffened fingers. You can

▲ Keeping the rock strata consistent makes sense of slopes and allows water features to appear perfectly natural.

▶ The rock strata should appear as natural as possible, merging together in places, whilst separating in others to form planting pockets.

use a wooden rammer, but hands are sensitive and can feel the 'give' of the soil. A well-made rock garden soil will take the ramming without becoming unduly compacted and it will not hurt you either.

Once a rock is thoroughly rammed into position, the next one to it can be laid in its bed. It should be as close as possible to the first, but because of the irregularity of rocks there will always be a gap between them. Into this you should ram soil as tightly as possible.

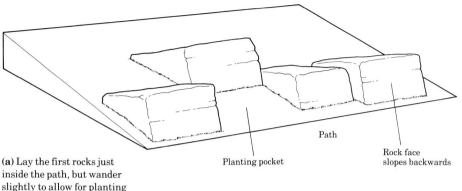

(a) Lay the first rocks just inside the path, but wander slightly to allow for planting pockets.

Fig. 8 Diagrammatic version of a rock garden under construction. The lowest layer has been laid first. The second layer in this design is a long way back, allowing for broad pockets and occasional rocks low down in the rock garden. This type of construction minimizes compaction of the surrounding soil.

Planting pocket

Path

Rock face slopes backwards

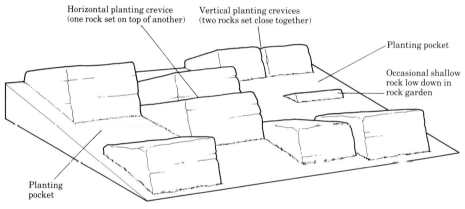

Horizontal planting crevice (one rock set on top of another)

Vertical planting crevices (two rocks set close together)

Planting pocket

Occasional shallow rock low down in rock garden

(b) The second layer can be set back from the course of the first layer and can wander to create further planting pockets.

Planting pocket

It is impossible to over-emphasize the importance of taking your time over thoroughly ramming the rocks into place. Jumping on them or kicking them in an attempt to set them firmly will simply not work and will leave you frustrated and possibly injured. Never be satisfied that you have finished with a rock until you can stand on it and it resists all your attempts to rock it. Only then will it be a suitable element in the environment you seek to create for the plants.

The second layer
You should aim in general for the first layer of rocks to wander slightly from the overall boundary of the rock garden, so that here and there a soil pocket is left inside the perimeter path and at its level (Fig. 8). If the path and the first layer of rocks coincide too closely there will be some loss of natural effect – not much, but enough that it is worth avoiding.

The second layer can wander quite substantially from the course of the first. In places, you may have a few rocks placed almost directly on top of those below, while in others the second layer is laid some distance behind the first, to wind forward again once more to join it. This creates flat soil pockets for mat-forming and spot plants.

However, you should always bear in mind the rock outcrop effect you are seeking. If the second and any subsequent layers of rock wander too much from the first, the illusion will be lost.

Layout in larger rock gardens

If your rock garden is going to be fairly large, the above system becomes expensive, as it is rock-intensive. On a larger scale, it is better to make several individual, quite small rock outcrops, separated by areas of scree or apparent scree (see pages 45–47).

These should be made to appear as though they thrust through the surrounding scree. In general they will present a sharp or fairly sharp angle, with the sides sweeping back into the scree.

This is the best method for a larger rock garden on a slope. On the flat, a combination of the larger, stratified rock outcrop and smaller ones separated by screes and paths is best.

Further layers of rock

It is a big mistake to make your rock garden into something monumental, approaching the stepped pyramids of Chitchen Itza. Don't go on adding layers of rock until a peak appears. A lower profile will be much more pleasing, and the flat upper surface can be broken up with individual rocks. Each of these should be quite large and well sunk, so make sure that you save a few suitable rocks for the purpose. It is here that the difference between a well-made and a brilliant rock garden will manifest itself. Very few rock gardens exist onto which we do not look downwards, and a flat expanse surrounded by a wall of rocks will not look natural.

The top should look as though it is the top of a solid mass of rock – again riven by fissures, but this time they can be quite wide – which has weathered and acquired a soil that has almost filled up the fissures.

In practice, of course, you will create pockets of soil, which you can make into different textures for different kinds of plants. The rock garden will not really be a solid but split piece of mountain, but it is extremely important that this is the illusion you create.

Crevice planting (Fig. 9)

Most people, when building a rock garden, leave the planting until the building is over. In fact, most good books and magazines advocate leaving things for two weeks or more to allow the soil to

· ROCK GARDEN SOILS ·	
Soil type	*Addition*
Sand	Garden compost
	Well-rotted manure
	Rotted straw
	Peat plus limestone chippings (peat alone is too acid). Use peat substitute if you are against the use of peat
	Buried stones (any kind)
Heavy clay	Garden compost
	Well-rotted manure
	Rotted straw
	Peat or substitute
	Gravel to one-fifth of the total bulk
Soft limestone (chalk in U.K.)	Generous amounts of any well-rotted organic material
	Limestone chippings to one-third of the total bulk
Medium loam	Gravel and small stones to one-third of the total bulk
All other light soils	As much well-rotted organic matter as possible

settle. This is excellent advice and should, with one exception, be followed. That exception is planting the tighter crevices, and this is something that is better done as you build.

The reason for this is that it is very difficult to get a pot-grown rock plant into a fissure or crevice without damaging it, and if you leave all the planting until later you will be reduced either to not planting the crevices at all or to pushing in seeds in the hope that they will germinate. This latter procedure is by no means a bad one. In fact,

Fig. 9 Crevice planting.

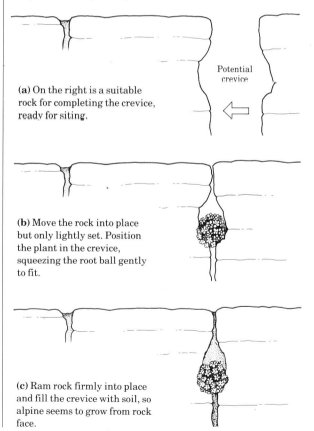

(a) On the right is a suitable rock for completing the crevice, ready for siting.

Potential crevice

(b) Move the rock into place but only lightly set. Position the plant in the crevice, squeezing the root ball gently to fit.

(c) Ram rock firmly into place and fill the crevice with soil, so alpine seems to grow from rock face.

it is to be recommended. However, there are plants, such as most of the named saxifrages, that you cannot grow from seed, and which you need to plant as plants.

When you have placed a rock and are about to butt the next one up to it, try it for shape. If it looks as though a nice, plantable crevice is going to result, put the second rock in position, but only partly firm it into position. Plant as follows:

1. Water your plant and remove it from its pot. Gently tease away the looser soil from around its collar, and – gently again, but quite firmly – squeeze the root ball so as to elongate it slightly.

2. Choose the spot on the first rock where the crevice is to be, and place the plant against it so that its above-ground parts are just clear of the rock surface and the roots are within the crevice.

3. Manoeuvre the second rock so that its side face butts onto the plant and allow it to flatten the root ball somewhat and hold it in position.

4. Proceed with ramming the soil round the second rock in order to fix it in position.

5. Ram soil into the crevice, making absolutely sure that there are no air pockets to dry out the roots of the plants and harbour pests. Fill the crevice around the root ball with rammed soil and, if it is wide enough, insert small pieces of stone beneath the foliage of the plant.

6. Water the plant. If you have done the job properly, only a very little superficial soil should be washed away.

Planning the planting
It is a bad idea to aim to produce a fully planted, instant effect. Whatever sort of garden you plant, you should always allow room for the plants to grow. This sounds like pretty elementary advice,

Planting pockets of iberis, sedums and dwarf conifers on a rock garden which has been neatly top-dressed with gravel, but leaves space for further growth.

but it is a sad fact that a very large proportion indeed of the problems gardeners have – including those involving pests and diseases – are caused by imprudent planting that allows for little in the way of growth.

In a rock garden this is extremely important, as overcrowding can be insidious and it can quite escape your notice that some choice little plant has been entirely swallowed up by a more vigorous neighbour until you find its soggy, brown corpse one day when cutting back the invader.

Fig. 10 Planting technique for alpines.

(a) Set plant at the same level as it was grown in the container.

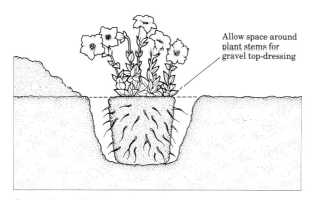

Allow space around plant stems for gravel top-dressing

(b) Top dress with a layer of gravel.

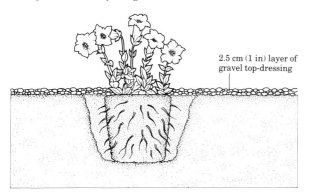

2.5 cm (1 in) layer of gravel top-dressing

Apart from planting the crevices, which as we have seen should be regarded as a separate job, the planting plan should be left until construction is complete. Then you can decide how you would like to plant the pockets, what dwarf conifers to put where, and so on.

This is where discipline comes in and you should plant considerably less than half the plants you think the rock garden requires. The reasons for this are:

1. You will thus be certain that you will have avoided overcrowding and the problems that stem from it.

2. It will give you time – a year or two – to learn about the plants and to realize what differences there are in growth between, say, a cushion saxifrage and a variety of *Phlox subulata*.

3. It is as certain as night follows day that you will become interested in rock plants and alpines and will in the near future come across far more fascinating ones than you ever imagined. However, you may not want to have to build a second rock garden yet!

Planting and top dressing
Much is written about planting techniques. As far as rock plants and alpines are concerned, forget it. There is really nothing to it. Make a hole with a trowel, knock the plant from its pot, put it in the hole, firm the soil round it, make it level, water it, and that's the job done.

Top dress the whole rock garden (except the rock faces of course) with about 3 cm (just over 1 in) of clean gravel to keep the plants and your boots clean, the soil cool and moist, weeds from germinating, and the necks of the plants dry (Fig. 10). Any weeds that do grow should be very easy to pull out.

· 4 ·
The Shady Side

You can if you wish build your rock garden entirely in shade, but it will be successful only if you plant it exclusively with plants that like or need shade. As most of them tend to have leaves that are quite large and flower stems that are relatively long, they will be likely to swamp the choice minority that do better in less vigorous company.

Shade and aspect

A planting in shade should be a celebration of shade, rather than a struggle to make the best of it, and a rock garden is essentially a feature on which the sun should be allowed to shine. Sunny pockets and shady nooks will exist side by side as a result of the way the rocks lie and the general direction (if any) the rock garden faces.

Of course a rock garden facing south (north in the southern hemisphere) will be sunnier than one facing any other direction. Even so, parts of it will be in shade for some of the day, even if it is only because the sides of some of the rocks are in shade in either the morning or the afternoon.

A rock garden built on the flat will have more shady places on its polar side than its equatorial aspect, but each will still provide a mixture of sun and shade. On a sunny slope there will be fewer shady positions, but there will still be some.

A larger rock garden can be built so that part of it is in the dappled shade of trees for most of the time, and this allows you to enjoy a change of character of the plantings within the rock garden.

Plants and shade

A great many plants that we come across in general gardening (including lilies and clematis, for example) are at their happiest when their roots and leaves are in shade but their flowers can reach the sun. The same applies to many rock plants. The point of this observation is that as long as their leaves are shaded, the flowering stems of shade-loving rock plants can be in sun.

Shade is not only to be used for plants whose natural habitat it is, but also for those that need shading from the sun during the hottest part of the day but which can enjoy it for the rest of the time. Generally speaking, the former prefer a more leafy, organic soil, while the latter are more at home if it is stonier and more gritty. In practice, however, the general rock garden soil you have made will do for all the plants you are likely to grow unless you become a serious enthusiast for alpines – not a bad fate, I may add.

One thing to remember with the shady parts of the rock garden is that they will become dry for much less of the time than the sunny areas. This makes drainage all the more important. If you have taken all the precautions to endure good drainage that you should, and have made your rock garden soil properly, there is no need to do

◀ *Viola hederacea* is a slightly tender plant for a cool, shady place. It must not be planted in a frost pockct.

▶ One of the most attractive aspects of the shady rock garden is the play of light and shade on the plants, which are more ferny and leafy than those growing in sunny places.

anything more. However, it is vital not to tread on the soil more than is absolutely necessary. In the more shady, moist pockets it is a good idea to lay in flat stepping stones. These will spread your weight over a wider area and there will be much less compaction of the soil underneath.

Shade-loving plants

There are more rock plants than you might think that are lovers of shade. Just about all of them will take a little sun, however. Their requirements are either for dappled shade from nearby trees or for the part shade that results from the rockwork.

Ramondas and haberleas are classic examples of shade-loving alpines. These are closely related to one another and distant cousins of African violets (*Saintpaulia* species). They have flat rosettes of overlapping leaves. In ramondas they are very flat and the leaves are wrinkled; in haberleas they are less flat, narrower and not as wrinkled. In the purple flowers of each you can see the likeness to the gloxinias and streptocarpus to which they are also related. They are, nevertheless, rock plants (alpines) and love to be in contact with rock. If you plant them on their sides in shady crevices they will live long and grow quite lush. Ramondas, in particular, have a quite amazing capacity for recovering after having shrivelled from drought.

Toughness of alpines

Alpines are, generally speaking, tough plants and this toughness only breaks down when those from the very highest mountain habitats become too wet in winter. I would fail the purpose of this book if I were to suggest for one moment that alpines and rock plants are hard to grow. They are not. Until you reach the rarified reaches of the enthusiast with his alpine house and frames, you

40

can relax in the knowledge that if these plants were not resilient, they would not survive in nature.

Nevertheless, you can't expect a shade lover to stand up to the scorching sun. This is not a sign of weakness in a plant; in all other respects but the provision of shade, it can be treated with respect but not cosseted.

Plants that need part shade

Among the alpines and rock plants that benefit from part shade there are two main groups:
- plants that will not be damaged by full sun but grow, flower or colour better in part shade.
- plants that can be damaged by full sun.

It has to be emphasized again that the strength of the sun varies with latitude, and that it is

impossible to be specific about what will benefit from part shade in different places. In general, though, it is reasonable to advise you that all the plants mentioned in this book will tolerate full or almost full sun in Scotland, while all of them will thrive better in part (dappled) shade in, say, North America's upper New York State.

In between (which means the greater part of England, and maritime climates such as the seaboard of the State of Washington), the plant groups in the chart on this page should be given shade during the hottest part of the day.

Effects of too much sun

What happens, for example, to most of the cushion saxifrages is that they burn if exposed to the sun during the middle of the day – say from 11 am to 3.30 pm – in all latitudes but the highest.

A mild case of burn is hardly noticeable. The cushion turns a lighter green, perhaps almost yellow in places, and flowering is greatly reduced. You are unlikely to link the poor flowering with sun because we are conditioned to expect that sunshine increases flowering in plants and because these plants flower early in the spring when we do not expect much in the way of sun.

A slightly worse case turns the cushions yellow on their sunniest sides, and the yellow patches usually turn brown eventually. In a bad case of scorching the brown, dead stage is reached rapidly. Even the toughest cushion saxifrages, such as *Saxifraga* × *apiculata*, will suffer unsightly burns in full sun.

· PLANTS FOR SHADE ·

1. Plants that benefit from shade during the hottest part of the day:

Androsaces	*Mentha requinii*
Dwarf astilbes	European primulas
Cyananthus	Dwarf rhododendrons
Dicentra	Cushion saxifrages
Spring and trumpet	Mossy saxifrages
gentians (*Gentiana verna*	Silver saxifrages
pontica and *G. acaulis*	Soldanellas
types)	Rock garden violas and
Hepatica	*Viola* species

2. Plants that enjoy shade – preferably dappled – for the greater part of the day:

Andromedas	Dodecatheons
Asiatic gentians	Gaultherias
Asiatic primulas	Haberleas
Cassiopes	Kalmias
Celmisias	Phyllodoces
Cortusas	Ramondas
Cyclamen	Trilliums

Planning for shade

If you have a good idea of the plants you want to grow, it makes sense deliberately to make shady environments for them as you build the rock garden. If, on the other hand, you are building without much of a structured notion yet of what the plants will be, then you should nevertheless make sure to provide shady nooks, as some of the ones that turn out to appeal to you will inevitably be among those that need some shade.

For example, a ramonda, which loves to grow vertically in a crevice, is easily provided for on the shady sides of some rocks. However, the spring gentian (*Gentiana verna pontica*) which likes to grow in a group on the flat, and which prefers shade during the middle of the day, needs different provision.

A soil pocket, well protected from the hot sun by rocks, will enjoy the shade cast at an angle to the sun by the rocks. The angle changes surprisingly quickly, and you will need to cater for this

Fig. 11 **Providing part shade in the middle of the day.**

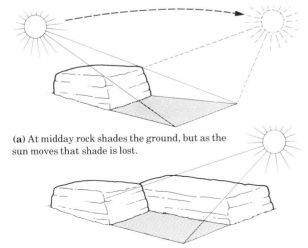

(a) At midday rock shades the ground, but as the sun moves that shade is lost.

(b) Another rock placed at an angle will increase the shade, giving a larger shady planting area.

so that morning and late afternoon sun reach the plants while the hotter sun of the middle of the day is kept from them.

This may sound complicated, but of course it is not, and can be expressed simply by saying that you can place the rocks so as to cast shade that will move during the day (Fig. 11).

The shady part of the rock garden

If part of your rock garden is permanently or almost permanently in shade, you have the chance to create a dramatic change of mood and enjoy a very different style of planting.

The main characteristics of the shady part that should be different from the sunnier areas of the rock garden are:

● *There will be much less rock.* This is because the plants are much leafier and also look much better when planted in groups. Most plants of the sunnier areas look good as single specimens and are set off by the rocks; those of the shady places look better when not interrupted by rock.

● *The rockwork will mainly be confined to defining changing levels.* In effect, the shady part of the rock garden is built more in a terraced fashion than as rock outcrop.

● *The soil surface should look 'woodsy' and not as if it were the top of a scree.* What this means is that you do without the top dressing of pebbles. It is not necessary, as the large leaves of the plants will not become soil-splashed, and the plants are not damaged by dampness.

A rock garden that is partly in sun and then runs into shade (but not the dry shade under dense trees) provides a natural habitat for an almost endless variety of plants. Because your space is limited, you will have to choose carefully, but in doing so you will enjoy yourself a great deal.

· 5 ·
Screes and Water

Many people think that scree is the gravelly or pebbly top-dressing given to rock gardens to protect against soil splash and collar-damp. In fact, it is much more than that – a deep, stony structure in which alpines and rock plants that are quite difficult to grow well in the ordinary rock garden soil can be made to thrive happily.

SCREES

In nature, a mountain scree can be of two kinds, stable and unstable. Unstable screes are usually relatively recent. They consist of stone slides, often at angles of about 40°, which give under the foot – sometimes most alarmingly – if you try to walk across them.

Stable screes are generally at a flatter angle and do not move underfoot. They are colonized with plants to a greater or lesser degree, and between the stones there is a very gritty soil. This is usually surprisingly rich, especially in mountains where chamois, ibex or goats live, and is, of course, perfectly drained. The plants send their roots a very long way in search of food and water. A cushion plant only 12 cm (5 in) across may well have a root system 1.8 m (6 ft) long.

A rock garden scree is a structure that provides the same kind of homes for plants as a stable scree in nature. It is easy to make, takes very little maintenance, and increases the quality and range of the plants you can grow. It should run down the rock garden almost like a river of stones, widening as it goes, and is more convincing when made to follow a winding or curving course between the rocks. The top layer should be of the same gravel as the top dressing of the rock garden as a whole – what will distinguish a well-made scree is not that its surface is different, but that it has been made so that the rocks alongside it define it. (I do not mean that you should even think of making a wall of rocks along its sides, but if you refer to the photograph opposite, you will see how the scree is implied, rather than emphasized.)

If your soil is excessively heavy, you can do what I did when I gardened on what had once been a potter's field, and make the entire rock garden into scree. In the main, though, it will be just one interesting feature of your rock garden.

Making a scree
The first step is to make the bed of the scree. This is a matter of taking out the rock garden soil to a depth of between 30 and 60 cm (12–24 in). Alternatively, you can allow for the scree bed as you build the rock garden.

The lighter your soil, the shallower the scree can be. As you will have made your rock garden soil properly, your garden soil, even if heavy,

◄ *Phormium* 'Bronze Baby', achilleas and other plants on a well-made scree.

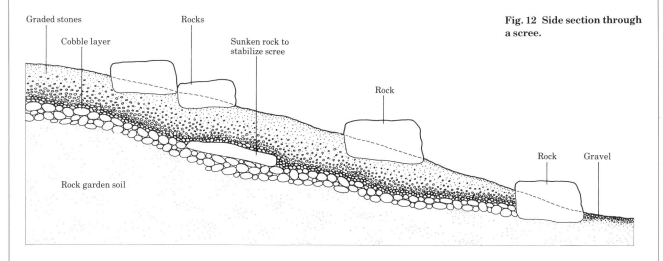

Graded stones

Cobble layer

Rocks

Sunken rock to stabilize scree

Rock

Rock   Gravel

Rock garden soil

Fig. 12 Side section through a scree.

should have been lightened and made workable, and anything more than a 60 cm (24 in) depth should really be unnecessary, except in rare, pure clay situations.

The scree bed should run downwards (Fig. 12), not only for aesthetic reasons, but also so that the water that drains through it can run away. An isolated scree on the flat becomes a sump (Fig. 13).

The scree consists of stones that are graduated from large cobbles at the bottom to gravel at the top. Twenty years and more ago you would have been advised, after laying the cobbles, to have covered them with a layer of 'drainage' material, consisting of inverted turves, coconut fibre, or the like. We do not do that any more, just as we do not put deep layers of broken crocks in flower pots. The reason is that we understand better how water moves in soils, especially gritty, stony ones. The principle is simply that of what goes up must come down – unless stopped somehow.

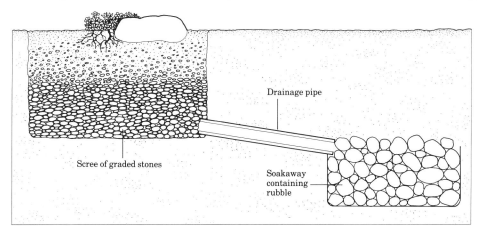

Drainage pipe

Scree of graded stones

Soakaway containing rubble

Fig. 13 Cross-section of a long scree built on the flat. In all but the lightest soils, a scree excavated on the flat will tend to be a sump. By putting in a drain and a soakaway, the sump is below the level of plant roots.

Make your scree soil from two-thirds stone and one-third of your rock garden soil. This is already gravelly, and to it you should add a double handful of sharp sand to the barrow-load. When mixed in, it will give an added texture to the soil, changing it to something like that of a sugary cake mixture with nuts in it. This kind of soil, known to alpine gardeners as 'gritty', is commonly prescribed for the slightly more tricky plants. When mixed with large amounts of stony material in a scree, it comes close to that found in nature.

The ideal way to proceed is to fill the scree bed by graduating the stones by using smaller ones in the mixture as you go. If this is a nuisance and your budget and inclinations lead you to using one grade of stone above the cobbles, do so by all means. The scree will be perfectly efficient.

Here and there, sink rocks into the scree, preferably shallow, flat ones. They will not only stabilize the scree but will also help to prevent it becoming dry in long spells of drought.

Over a long period, the nutrients in the soil will tend to be leached away. To combat this, lightly scatter sieved garden compost or leaf mould over the surface of the scree each autumn.

· PLANTS SUITABLE FOR THE SCREE ·

Androsaces	*Gentiana verna pontica*
Aquilegia bertolonii	*Helichrysum milfordiae*
A. discolor	*Phlox douglasii* varieties
Armeria caespitosa	*Phyteuma comosum*
Asperula lilacaeflora caespitosa	*Potentilla nitida*
Campanula allionii	Saxifrages – silver and cushion types*
C. arvatica	*Vitaliana primuliflora*
Dianthus – dwarf and cushion types	Dwarf narcissi, irises, crocuses and cyclamen are also ideal.
Drabas	
Edraianthus pumilio	*Plant where there is shade in the hottest part of the day.
Erodiums (dwarf)	

WATER IN THE ROCK GARDEN

There is nothing quite as pleasant in a rock garden design as an associated water feature. The sight and sound of water is peaceful and always fascinating, and its presence brings a cooler, moister atmosphere which is appreciated by the plants. However, there are a few do's and don'ts about water features in a rock garden that are so important it is worth stating them at the outset:

1. *Don't* have a water feature whose starting point is high up on a rock garden built on the flat. You have to ask where it would have come from in nature.

2. *Don't* spoil a perfectly natural-looking rock garden with a water course whose artificial nature is glaringly obvious.

3. *Don't* install an artificial-looking fountain or piece of statuary when you have striven to make a natural rock garden.

4. *Don't* harbour ambitions to keep Koi carp in a rock garden pool – they need deep water and special conditions.

5. *Don't* attempt to install electrical apparatus out of doors unless you are a qualified electrician. It is *not* good enough to be 'handy'.

6. *Do* think twice before installing anything other than a simple pond – and then think again.

7. *Do* make ponds and pools large and deep enough. Shallow, small pools heat up quickly, contain little oxygen, and soon fill up with algae. If you haven't enough room for a fair-sized pond, don't go in for water at all.

The ideal situation for a water-associated rock garden is on a slope, where it is possible to have a pond at the lowest level, with a rock bank behind

▲ The arrangement of the rocks on this grassy slope not only makes it appear as if the rock outcrop was natural, but also lends logic to the pond's existence.

◀ A small waterfall always adds interest to the rock garden.

it, from which a streamlet appears to spring and feed the pond.

Hybrids of the artificial and the natural always look wrong, and it is much the best plan to keep the whole thing as simple as possible. Remember, too, that your rock garden is going to be made with the plants as the first consideration: this should extend to the water feature.

Making a pond (Fig. 14)

Constructing a pond is simplicity itself these days. Use a length of rope to 'draw' it on the ground, and then peg the rope down. Dig the pond out, leaving a shelf about 22 cm (9 in) below the surface for marginal plants. Slope the sides gently and line them with 2.5 cm (1 in) of sand, making sure that nothing sharp projects through the sand.

Now measure the maximum length and the maximum width of the pond. Also measure the maximum depth, which should be between 60 and 90 cm (24–36 in).

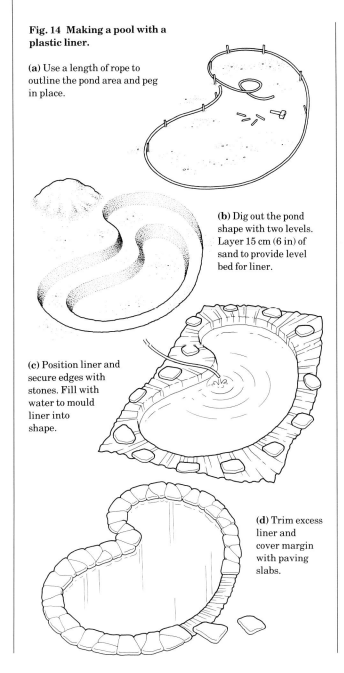

Fig. 14 Making a pool with a plastic liner.

(a) Use a length of rope to outline the pond area and peg in place.

(b) Dig out the pond shape with two levels. Layer 15 cm (6 in) of sand to provide level bed for liner.

(c) Position liner and secure edges with stones. Fill with water to mould liner into shape.

(d) Trim excess liner and cover margin with paving slabs.

Buy as stout and durable a pond liner as you can possibly afford (butyl is best, and comes in different grades). According to this formula:

1. The length of the liner should be the maximum (i.e. overall) length of the pool *plus* twice the maximum depth.

2. The width of the liner should be the maximum (i.e. overall) width of the pool *plus* twice the maximum depth.

Thus a pool 3.6 m × 2.55 m (12 ft × 8 ft) and 60 cm (24 in) deep will need a liner 4.8 m × 3.75 m = 18 sq m; or 16 ft × 12ft = 192 sq ft (21.3 sq yd).

Lay the liner in and anchor it with stones at the edges. Let the water in slowly and pull out any wrinkles as they form.

The excavated soil

It is not a good idea to dig out a pond and then use the soil for the rock garden. This flies in the face of the rock garden being primarily a home for plants, as you will be almost certain to dig up a lot of subsoil, which is useless – even harmful – to plants. Use the top spit soil by all means, but no more. It is worth the hire of a skip to get rid of the unwanted subsoil, rather than try to make something of it in the garden.

Whatever gardening you are doing, keep an eye on the difference between topsoil and subsoil. The only way to improve the latter is by breaking it up and mixing it with organic material.

Watercourses

If you have thought twice about adding anything other than a simple pond, and have decided even so that you would like to enjoy the sight and sound of running water, then you must be prepared to spend extra money, planning-time and building effort in getting it right.

You *can* use pre-formed plastic watercourse sections, but they do not blend in well with rock and, while they save a good deal of labour, they never really look anything other than artificial. Your watercourse is better made using butyl liner held in place by rocks laid so as to form part of the natural strata of the rock garden.

Choosing a pump (Fig. 15)

The flow of water should be enough to hide the liner. A watercourse that is too wide for the delivered flow looks artificial and wrong.

Years ago, you might have been advised to hook up a hose to an outside tap, from which your watercourse could be run as required. We have come a long way since then both in terms of standards of garden design and in our notions of water as a resource that should not be wasted.

Nowadays water features are almost always pump-driven. A small, narrow watercourse or a simple, short waterfall at the pond's edge can be driven by a submersible pump. This lies actually in the pond and circulates water to the head of the feature. A larger affair requires a surface pump, which should be enclosed in a dry concrete chamber near to the head of the watercourse.

Fig. 15 Circulation in water features.

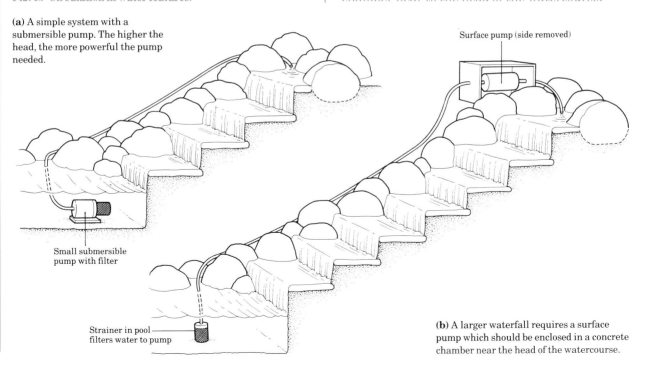

(a) A simple system with a submersible pump. The higher the head, the more powerful the pump needed.

Surface pump (side removed)

Small submersible pump with filter

Strainer in pool filters water to pump

(b) A larger waterfall requires a surface pump which should be enclosed in a concrete chamber near the head of the watercourse.

A surface pump and its chamber will take up too much room in a small rock garden, but in a larger one it can be made unobtrusive. Surface pumps are more expensive than submersible ones. For both kinds you can buy kits complete with strainers and all the necessary valves.

Please remember that water and electricity are a lethal mix. This is one of the reasons why you should always think carefully before installing a watercourse. Nothing looks worse than a watercourse that is not running, and you need to set up a routine so that it is switched on, say, whenever you go out of the door into the garden. Engage a professional electrician.

Suitable water plants

Although we want to achieve a natural appearance, any garden is a compromise and we have to live in a real world where feet cause grass to wear, washing has to be hung out, and children play. You will, therefore, be likely to have a path round your rock garden, which may be quite near the garage and may have the straight line of a fence behind it. None of these occur in nature. What matters, though, is that you make your compromise as far on the side of a natural home for the plants as you can.

This means not growing bulrushes or tall water irises in a pond near which are plants adapted to keeping their heads down out of the mountain gales, but it also means enjoying hybrid waterlilies that you would never see in a lifetime of mountain walking.

Water lilies vary greatly in their vigour and in the depth at which they like to grow. *Nymphaea* 'Caroliniana Nivea', for example, is a small water lily for water no deeper than 30 cm (12 in). Another white one, 'Gladstoniana', is so vigorous that it is capable of taking over a small lake.

Grow the water-lilies classified as 'medium' if your pond is between 7.5 and 14 sq m (80–150 sq ft) in area, and those listed as 'small' if it is less than this size.

Don't plant water-lilies where they are likely to be affected by the movement of water entering the pond from a watercourse or waterfall. Water-lilies must have still or nearly still water.

Oxygenating plants are important and you need to allow them a week or two to work before planting anything else. Plant the margins generously. See pages 90–93 for a selection of water plants.

◀ One of the many fine red water-lily varieties available for rock-garden ponds.

·6·

Troughs, Sinks and Walls

Wherever you read about rock gardens and alpine plants you will come across mentions of 'troughs and sinks'. It must be quite difficult for someone new to gardening to fathom what all the fuss is about – what are troughs and sinks and what use are they?

TROUGHS AND SINKS

Simply, what is being referred to here is merely growing rock and alpine plants in containers. It just so happens that the most congenial containers – the ones that suit the looks of the plants best and which most readily fit in with the rock garden landscape – are the old stone water troughs you used to find in farmyards and under water pumps, and the old, wide, shallow stone sinks that used to be common in houses.

The trouble is that most of them have been snapped up long ago. If you happen to find one, you are very lucky: if it is in an auctioneer's catalogue, be prepared to pay a lot of money.

You should not be put off by this, however, as it is perfectly possible to make highly acceptable substitutes, and we will come to how in a moment. Meanwhile, let us assume that you have a suitable trough, just so that we can look at the best way of making it into a small alpine garden. The other question to be answered is, 'Why bother?', and that is the one to be answered first.

The advantages of containers
Rock gardening is different from other forms of gardening. You become involved with a whole world of small plants and their specialized environment, and it can capture your interest much more than you might at first think.

If you make a dash for growth and plant masses of fast-growing mat-forming plants, or if the rockwork itself is the be-all and end-all, you will soon become bored with the whole thing. On the other hand, if you follow the advice of this book, which is that the plants come first, you will find a growing interest in the small, the choice, the dainty and the intriguing – all of which may find the rough and tumble of even the most well-regulated rock garden a little daunting.

An isolated environment, in which there is no chance of a little plant becoming swamped by a rapacious neighbour, has obvious advantages. Perhaps even more importantly, however, it affords you complete control.

The container environment
With a container you control the soil content and you are able to provide perfect drainage. You can also, if you wish, provide the container with a cover against excessive winter wet. Pick up a book written for alpine gardeners and you can read all about special structures – frames and alpine houses – for the more choice plants. But

53

Fig. 16 A glazed sink, showing how the compost can take up all the room inside as long as it is well drained. The drainage holes need to be covered – but not blocked – to stop the compost running out. A curved piece of broken clay flower pot or crockery is best.

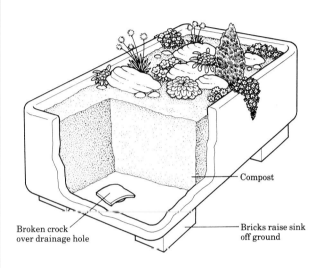

Compost

Broken crock over drainage hole

Bricks raise sink off ground

you can rest assured that with a few containers you will be able happily to grow almost as wide a range of plants as those who have all the specialist equipment.

Drainage (Fig. 16)

Whatever your trough is made of, it must have drainage holes in the bottom, preferably one for every 20 cm (8 in) run. They should be covered so that the compost does not run out, and this can be done with upturned, curved shards of broken pots or crockery or with discs cut from fine mesh, of which perforated zinc is best.

There is absolutely no need, as long as your compost is open and gritty, for any of the layers of 'crocks', 'drainage material', or various concoctions of leaves and 'upturned turves' that were the knee-jerk devices of yesteryear. If the compost

is well drained, so is the trough. If the bottom of the trough is uneven, make drainage holes where it is deepest.

Soils for troughs and sinks

The best way of making the compost is to buy a soil-based, John Innes type and then mix it 50/50 with a mixture which is itself 50/50 fine gravel and gritty sand. You will find all sorts of wondrous concoctions recommended elsewhere, but this works and does not involve unnecessary labour.

If your garden soil is limy, you can provide an environment for lime haters by making your compost from a 50/50 mixture of ericaceous compost and lime-free gravel and sand. This compost is based on peat or peat substitutes and is much too soggy when used on its own in a trough.

Placing a trough or sink

Where to put your rock plant container is largely a matter of taste, but there are a few factors that are important:

1. Decide where to site the trough or sink before you attempt to fill it. It is likely to be quite heavy enough before being full of soil.

2. Place it on supports. These need only be low – say the height of one house brick – but give you the chance to make certain the trough is level. When raised a little above the ground, it is also out of the reach of many pests.

3. Use a spirit level – a trough that is not precisely level cannot drain. This is the cause of most failures.

4. Place it on a path or paved area and away from tall plants or any source of rain drip. A trough placed on soil can all too soon find itself encroached upon by weeds. Alternatively, though, you can gravel over the soil.

· PLANTS FOR TROUGHS AND SINKS ·

Name	Description
Allium sikkimense	15 cm (6 in); blue flowers in summer.
Aquilegia bertolonii	8 cm (3 in); blue flowers in late spring.
Campanula arvatica	5 cm (2 in); blue flowers in summer.
Campanula cochlearifolia	8 cm (3 in); blue flowers in summer.
Cytisus decumbens	Prostrate; yellow flowers in late spring.
Dianthus alpinus	8 cm (3 in); rose-pink flowers in summer.
Dianthus 'La Bourboule'	5 cm (2 in); pink flowers in late spring.
Erodium chamaedryoides 'Roseum'	2.5 cm (1 in); rose flowers all summer.
Gentiana verna portica	2.5 cm (1 in); blue flowers in late spring.
Oxalis enneaphylla	5 cm (2 in); pink or rose flowers in early summer.
Potentilla nitida 'Rubra'	2.5 cm (1 in); rose flowers in early summer.
Saxifrages – cushion types	Spring-flowering.
Saxifraga cochlearis 'Minor'	8 cm (3 in); white flowers in late spring.
Sempervivums – smallest species	Rosettes of succulent pointed leaves; tiny flowers.
Vitaliana primuliflora	5 cm (2 in); yellow flowers in early summer.

Dwarf conifers

Chamaecyparis obtusa 'Nana'	60 × 75 cm (24 × 30 in) after 30 years; twisted sprays of black green.
Juniperus communis 'Compressa'	30 cm (12 in) after 10 years; very small pillar.
Cryptomeria japonica 'Vilmoriniana'	20 × 30 cm (8 × 12 in) after 12-15 years; bronze-green.

Old troughs from new (Fig. 17)

The old stone sinks were superseded by glazed ones, some of which were shallow, while others were deep and more like troughs. These look out of place in the garden, especially anywhere near the rock garden, but there is a way of making them appear old and as if made from well-weathered stone.

1. Make up a mixture of one part each of sand, cement, and sphagnum peat from which the coarser elements have been sieved away. The mixture should have the consistency of oatmeal porridge or grits (if you can bear such a thought).

2. Site the sink and level it. Clean it thoroughly with a grease solvent, dry, and then coat it with a layer of bonding adhesive.

3. Apply the mixture to the surfaces of the sink, using a trowel or plastic-gloved hand or both. You should let it extend down the inside to below where the soil level will be.

4. Cover with a moist sack, tarpaulin or heavy cloth, but not plastic. This allows it to dry slowly without cracking.

5. Before it is really dry, wire-brush it to remove angles and lumps and to make it look more like stone. Return the covering until the mixture is fully cured. Once the mixture is thoroughly dry, you can fill and plant your 'old' sink.

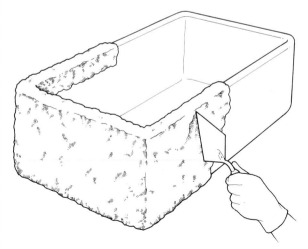

Fig. 17 Glazed sinks can be made to look much like old stone, and more fitting for the garden, by the application of 'hypertufa'.

▲ Vertical view of a trough, landscaped with sandstone and planted with small, choice alpines, including *Rhodohypoxis baurii*.

◄ With just one sink garden and a few pots, you can enjoy the world of alpine plants and rock gardening even in the smallest of spaces.

► *Sedum spathulifolium* 'Purpureum' is ideal for growing in troughs and sinks.

A completely artificial trough

You can manufacture a sink or trough from scratch using the mixture described above, which is called hypertufa. It involves making a simple mould from cardboard boxes and is very easy to do (Fig. 18). One box sits inside the other and the gaps between them are filled with hypertufa. The main thing is to see that the boxes do not collapse, and that presents no difficulty if you use old bricks or blocks to hold the sides of the outer box in place, while the inner box is filled with dry soil or sand.

The steps in construction after you have made the hypertufa mix are as follows:

1. Fill the bottom of the outer box with 5 cm (2 in) of hypertufa mixture. Place two or more pieces of broom handle dowelling 5 cm long in the mixture.

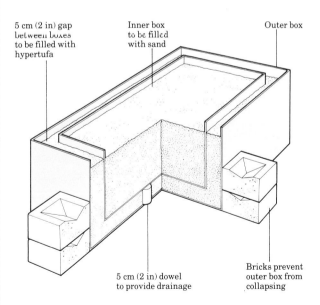

5 cm (2 in) gap between boxes to be filled with hypertufa

Inner box to be filled with sand

Outer box

5 cm (2 in) dowel to provide drainage

Bricks prevent outer box from collapsing

Fig. 18 A simple mould made from cardboard boxes. Only one 'hypertufa' trough or sink can be made from each mould, as the cardboard will have to be torn away before final hardening of the mixture.

These, when eventually knocked out, will leave drainage holes.

2. Place the smaller box inside. It should be of such a size as to leave a 5 cm (2 in) gap between it and the larger box.

3. Fill the gap with hypertufa and the inside of the smaller box with soil or sand so that the levels of each rise together.

4. Throughout, tamp the mixture down well and make sure there are no air pockets.

5. Cover with damp sacking, wire brush when half cured, and remove the sacking when the trough or sink is entirely cured.

Hypertufa mix can be artificially aged by painting it with sour milk or the product of soaking a bag of manure in a bucket. It will rapidly attract mosses and lichens and begin to look respectably ancient.

Planting a trough or sink

Many years ago, a television gardening programme showed an earnest host planting up a trough. In a very few minutes it was not just full but overflowing with plants, every one of which would have completely taken over the trough within two years.

This 'instant gardening' approach was unfair to the viewers. You will avoid disappointment if you choose the very smallest, daintiest plants for your troughs and sinks – the ones that are worthy of occupying such an exclusive residence.

Rock gardening within the small world of the sink, trough or other container is subject to exactly the same principles as it is on a larger scale. Rock, laid so as to simulate a natural outcrop, will look remarkably appropriate even in such an artificial situation.

Rocks play an important part in keeping the compost moist and cool. It is easy enough to water a trough, but you have to be there and it is all too easy for it to dry out while you are away on holiday. A few small rocks and a good top dressing of gravel will go a long way to preventing this.

On the small scale of the trough, it is easy to move the rocks around as you plant. You can place a plant firmly and then shift the positions of the rocks so that it appears to have grown between them.

Feeding

Normally, rock plants and alpines need little feeding beyond an annual scattering of hoof and horn or bonemeal (never the two together; the lime in the bonemeal causes the nitrogen in the hoof and horn to be lost as ammonia). In containers, however, it helps gently to remove as much of the top layer of soil as possible without unduly disturbing the plants and replace it with fresh soil.

An occasional weak liquid feed, applied to the whole trough, will do good, but it is worse to overdo it than omit it. A trough, sink, or other container of alpines should be a long-term home for them, not a short-term lodging.

RAISED BEDS

A raised bed is really just a very large trough. It has many of the advantages of a trough or sink. You have a great deal of control over the soil and the watering, and can easily make it possible to cover the bed in winter.

It is not portable, though, and a stone-built raised bed can be a matter for regret after it has been built in the wrong position. Planning, thinking and re-thinking are highly advisable.

There are several sound reasons for making raised beds for rock and alpine plants:

1. They cut out the inevitable bending and kneeling that a rock garden involves and are thus ideal for the elderly. Sensibly made, they are perfect for the disabled and chair-bound.

2. They bring plants to nose and eye level. The advantage of the former is obvious, when small pinks, violets and daphnes may have their perfumes readily appreciated. The latter is less so, but not to wearers of bifocal glasses, who find it difficult to see the fine points of small flowers at ground level.

3. It is much easier to cater for lime-hating plants in a limy garden with a raised bed than with containers. Dwarf rhododendrons, kalmiopsis, phyllodoces and so on can be grown to perfection in a raised, slightly shaded bed of lime-free soil even when the surrounding land is highly alkaline.

By the way, take no notice whatever of those who tell you that you must save rainwater for watering lime-haters in hard-water areas. As long as the compost is peaty and acid, it will not make the slightest difference if you water with the local, limy water. This is not opinion, but fact, backed up by many years of commercially producing lime-hating plants using lime-laden water.

59

Building a raised bed

A raised bed can be made from any materials that suit the garden – stone, bricks, or even heavy timber. If possible, leave small gaps in the sides. This involves leaving out a brick or adjusting the stone accordingly. The purpose is to provide the equivalent of the crevices in the rock garden, but you may feel that quite ordinary plants – such as aubrietas and alpine phloxes – will do a good job of decorating the sides of the bed.

◀ Alpines in and beside a raised bed, including *Dianthus* 'Icomb' and *Alyssum serpyllifolium*.

▲ Near-vertical banks of retaining walls such as this are frequent features in larger gardens. They are seldom planted imaginatively, as this one has been, using tumbling and mat-forming rock plants.

With raised beds of more than 60 cm (24 in) in depth, there is no need to fill them completely with soil. The lower third or so may consist of rubble or cobbles (lime free if necessary). This is not to provide 'drainage', but merely a practical device to lessen the need for finding soil. As with a trough, as long as the compost is well drained, the whole bed will be, too.

If you make the back of the bed higher than the front and slope the sides to the angle so formed, you will be able to put a frame light over the whole or part of it during wet winter weather. You should, however, allow for the height of the plants, and any rockwork should have a low profile.

WALLS

Walls are ideal places in which to grow rock and alpine plants – but not all walls. Gaps in a regular house wall are not places for plants, but sites for repair.

Old outbuildings, made of brick or stone, look romantic when supporting populations of plants, but most of us don't have them. If you do, though,

Fig. 19 Building a retaining wall.

The face of the wall should tilt slightly backwards. Use a long straight-edge and check the angle constantly

Each individual stone should also tilt backwards and downwards into the bank

Drive the occasional long stone deep into the bank for stability

Bond the stones on the face by overlapping them brick-fashion

Provide a deep, hardcore foundation

try the little, shrubby aethionemas like 'Warley Rose', or make mud pellets with seeds of *Erinus alpinus* and squash them into the gaps.

Dividing walls

If you have thought of making a low wall as a divider between parts of the garden – such as between the lawn and a flower bed, or separating the ornamental and the vegetable garden – it can be an ideal home for alpines and rock plants. All you have to do is to make it double instead of single and provide soil between. In fact, you are making a narrow raised bed.

A wall retaining a steep bank of soil or the abutments of a flight of steps is also ideal. It provides, in fact, a whole series of vertical and horizontal crevices and can be the most exciting form of rock garden, with exotic and unusual alpines enjoying life enormously in a situation where there is never dampness lying about their collars.

When you decide to make a retaining wall (Fig. 19), you should pay attention to two main considerations. These are:

1. The principles of good rock garden building still apply, and you should have a supply of properly made rock garden soil ready to use between and behind the stones or rocks, which will need to be rammed in the same way as was described on pages 32 and 34.

2. The principles of wall-building apply as well. The potential forces acting on a retaining wall are strong, and if ignored, will bring it down.

You will find it helpful to plant many of the plants as you build, but it is easy for those lower down to be damaged as you work higher up, and you need to take extra care. However, it is by no means difficult to leave spaces in a larger wall big enough to receive pot-grown alpines.

· 7 ·
Propagation and Aftercare

The art of propagating plants is a very old one indeed. Gardeners appear always to have gone in for increasing the numbers of their own plants to give to or exchange with friends.

Among rock gardeners you will find a great deal of swapping and giving of 'slips' or 'roots' of plants. In fact, a great many of the very best alpine and rock plants circulate in this manner rather than finding their way into commercial catalogues.

There are really very few gardeners at all who do not propagate plants in one way or another. Vegetable gardeners cannot grow much in the way of variety without raising plants from seed, and those who want an interesting array of summer bedding will soon find themselves bored with whatever bedding plants are usually on offer and will also resort to growing from seed.

An interesting, well-stocked rock garden will be quite expensive to run unless you go in for a certain amount of propagation. But economics are by no means the whole of the story. Propagating plants – especially alpines and rock plants – is among the most joyous of pastimes: the annual repetition of what even the most hardened of nurserymen still regard as miracles.

Basic principles
There are several different techniques, and all of them are simple and easily learned, even though you may hear all sorts of complicated old wives' tales about them. There are two essential principles upon which the whole of propagation depends, and if you remember these you will not go far wrong:

1. Plants have a lust for life, not a death wish. Built into them is a need to live, backed up by many millions of years of evolution. You have to do something very wrong to prevent it.

2. All plants depend on one rule: water lost by the leaves must never exceed water gained by the roots.

GROWING FROM SEED

The great majority of alpines and rock plants come from cold places and do not need heat to help them to germinate. Most, indeed, need to experience alternating cold and warmer spells so that they may 'know' that winter has gone, spring has arrived, and it is now safe to come up.

Thus the best time to sow your seeds is in autumn and the best place is in pots in a cold frame. By doing this, you allow the seeds to experience the chills of winter and the warming up that comes early in spring.

This works well for seed you have collected from your own plants or any that you might have been given, but seed that arrives in spring from

◄ Propagating material can be passed on to friends at almost any time of the year. Just a few cuttings will not be missed by well-grown plants.

► *Geranium* 'Ballerina' is easily propagated using root cuttings (see chart on page 67).

commercial suppliers has been stored dry and at an even temperature and has no knowledge of the passing of winter.

Spring sowing

There are all sorts of techniques for breaking the dormancy of seeds that are still waiting for the right signals. You may be advised to put the pots of seed in the fridge, for example. That is all very well, but domestic harmony may not survive such practices.

Patience is the best technique of all. Sow your rock plant and alpine seed whenever you obtain it, put it in your cold frame, keep it watered and weeded and wait. If it does not come up in the first year it almost certainly will in the second. Don't throw away any pots of seed until it has gone three years without producing any seedlings.

Sowing techniques

Don't worry about all the various recipes for composts you may have heard about. Buy some soil-based seed compost of the John Innes type, mix it 50/50 by volume with sharp grit (the sort sold for adding to the feed of newly hatched poultry is ideal), put it in the pots, firm it down, and you are ready to go.

Sow the seeds on the surface of the compost. If they are larger seeds, press them down gently; otherwise leave them alone. Cover them with a layer of small gravel or the sort of grit sold for turkeys, to a depth of about 1.5 cm (just over ½ in). Water either with several quick passes of a fine-rosed watering can or by partly immersing the pots in water until the top dressing turns dark.

The final job is to put a clearly and indelibly written label in each pot, with the name of the plant and the date of sowing – don't forget the year.

And that, believe it or not, really is all there is to raising alpines and rock plants from seed.

DIVISION

Simple division is the easiest of all methods of propagating rock garden plants, but it cannot be applied to all of them. Those with a single stem, such as *Geranium* 'Ballerina', dwarf shrubs, and any plants that do not make several growing points or crowns at ground level cannot be divided and must be raised by other means.

That still leaves a good many, however, including many of the mainstay plants such as campanulas, some dianthus, many primulas and the lime-hating asiatic gentians. The actual technique varies almost from plant to plant, but two examples cover most of what you will encounter.

Multi-crowned plants (Fig. 20a)

The little *Primula warshenewskyana*, for instance, a plant beauty in miniature saddled with a sneeze of a name but perfect for a partly shaded trough, is typical of plants with close-packed, multiple crowns.

Lift the plant in mid-spring and hold it in your hands in a bucket of water. Gently swish it to and fro while, also gently, kneading the root ball between your fingers. The soil will wash away quite quickly.

The crowns will begin to separate, and with some careful teasing will come apart, providing you with a surprising number of little plants. You can plant the larger ones straight away, while the smaller offsets can be potted up to grow on in a frame for a year.

Plants with wandering stems (Fig. 20b)

These form the other main group and require a different method. *Campanula cochlearifolia* is typical. You need not lift the whole plant. Two years or more after planting, you will find that the plant has wandered, making little patches of foliage. In mid-spring, drive your trowel straight down between one of the furthest patches and its nearest neighbour and lift it. It will come up as a

Fig. 20 Dividing multi crowned plants and plants with wandering stems.

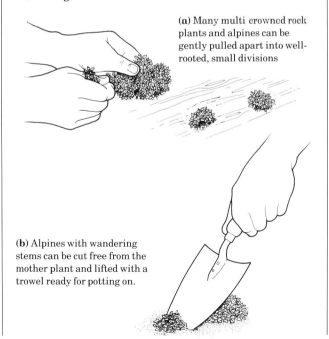

(a) Many multi crowned rock plants and alpines can be gently pulled apart into well-rooted, small divisions

(b) Alpines with wandering stems can be cut free from the mother plant and lifted with a trowel ready for potting on.

separated plant, which you can now unravel in water to reveal several thready stems, each with a supply of roots. Pull these apart, and pot them up to grow on.

SOFTWOOD CUTTINGS – OR SEMI-RIPE?

Many more alpines are grown from softwood cuttings than are shrubs or herbaceous perennials. Their size is on their side for, as you will remember, water lost by the leaves must not exceed water gained by the root. A cutting is in effect a plant with no roots at all and therefore with an ability to take up water limited by the capillary action of its stem. Larger cuttings with larger leaves lose water much more rapidly than the average alpine, which is small by comparison.

Furthermore, a large number of alpines and rock plants flower quite early in the year and make their new growth very quickly. This means that you can take softwood cuttings before the hot weather gets under way – and the loss of water will be less than it would be later. A shrub, whose leaves are larger and which makes its growth later than many alpines, may be difficult to manage as a softwood cutting because of the higher temperatures and the larger leaves that conspire to cause rapid water loss.

With alpines that make their growth later in the season, you often have a choice of soft or semi-ripe cuttings. These latter are fully described below, but are less given to wilting as the stems are firmer and the leaves, being more mature, have tougher outer layers and lose water less readily.

Softwood cuttings (Fig. 21)
A good example of a typical subject for propagating from softwood cuttings is *Phlox douglasii* in any of its varieties. As the last few flowers are

· A YEAR OF PROPAGATION ·	
Season	*Action*
Early winter	Root cuttings of *Morisia monanthos*, *Anchusa caespitosa* and *Geranium* 'Ballerina'; lift the plant, remove a thick root, cut into pieces 2.5 cm (1 in) long, and set vertically in 50/50 peat and sand in a pot in a frame; pot individually in late spring when well developed.
Late winter and early spring	Sow seeds of alpines and rock plants in pots in a cold frame.
Mid- and late spring	Pot up seedlings and take softwood cuttings of early-flowering alpines.
Early and mid-summer	Continue potting seedlings and pot up cuttings as they root; don't forget to water and mist-spray the cuttings during the rooting process.
Late summer	Take semi-ripe cuttings of later-flowering and shrubby alpines and rock plants.
Early autumn	Continue to take semi-ripe cuttings and pot up those that have rooted.
Mid- and late autumn	Sow seed of your own harvesting or any that come your way, and leave to germinate in a cold frame over winter; inspect them at least once a week.

about to fade, the appearance of the mat of foliage will subtly change. Instead of being uniformly darkish green there will be points of light green where the new shoots are coming through. Follow one of these down and you will find that it is about 2.5 cm (1 in) long and very soft. The procedure for taking the cutting is as follows:

1. Take a very sharp knife – a razor blade is better – and cut off a new shoot just below a leaf joint. Take a few more and put them all in a plastic bag as you do so.

67

2. Have already prepared a clay pot containing a mixture of two-thirds sharp sand and one-third moss peat, ready watered. Take a cutting, leaving the rest in the closed bag, and remove its lowest pair of leaves by cutting down onto a block of wood (pulling the leaves off damages the soft bark of the cutting, and holding the cutting in the hand while using a sharp blade is not sensible). If the cutting is a long one, you may need to remove two pairs or possibly more.

Fig. 21 Taking softwood cuttings.

(**a**) A softwood cutting is taken just below a leaf joint.

(**b**) The lower leaves should be removed cleanly by cutting down onto a block of wood.

(**c**) Using a dibber, plant the cutting so that the bottom pair of leaves sit on the surface. Place in a partly shaded frame.

· HANDY TIP ·

Always set cuttings in soil with a blunt-ended 'dibber', such as an unsharpened diary pencil. If it is pointed, the end of the cutting may not reach the bottom of the hole and will be 'hung'. Hung cuttings do not root.

3. Insert the cutting into the mixture so that the next pair of leaves sits comfortably on it, and complete the procedure with the rest of the cuttings. Label the pot and put it in a closed, draught-free frame, preferably facing west or south-west (i.e. where it has warm sun but not all day) and shaded with white greenhouse shade paint.

4. All cuttings should be watered with a fine rose night and morning as necessary to keep a humid atmosphere and to keep the compost mixture damp.

5. The cuttings should be rooted in anything from five to fourteen days.

Semi-ripe cuttings (Fig. 22)
The procedure with semi-ripe cuttings is essentially the same. It is the selection of the cuttings that differs.

A good example is the dwarf shrub, *Penstemon davidsonii*. The shoots are not very much longer than they are with the phlox, but you will find them ready in late summer, when they will be becoming woody,

They should not be so woody as to snap if you try to bend them, neither should they be so soft as to be bent right back on themselves without

▶ *Phlox douglasii* 'Rosea' (bottom left), growing here with *Daphne cneorum* 'Eximia', is propagated by softwood cuttings.

Fig. 22 Taking semi-ripe cuttings.

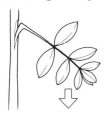

(a) Taking a semi-ripe cutting with a heel of old wood.

(b) Using a sharp knife, neatly trim back the ragged end, leaving a short spur.

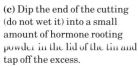

(c) Dip the end of the cutting (do not wet it) into a small amount of hormone rooting powder in the lid of the tin and tap off the excess.

(d) Insert the stem to about half its length in a 50/50 mixture of peat and sand.

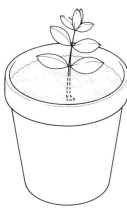

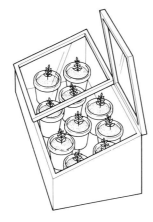

(e) The more cuttings you make, the fuller your frame will be. This makes for a humid atmosphere and produces much better results than if the frame is less full.

breaking. Somewhere in between, they are known as 'semi-ripe'.

There are two ways of taking them. The first is to cut them just below a leaf joint, as you do with softwood cuttings. The second is to take them with a 'heel' of the old wood. To do this, grip the cutting firmly near its base and pull it down parallel to the main stem. It will come away with a sliver of old wood. Tidy the sliver with your knife or razor, so that a roughly triangular 'heel' is left at the base of the cutting. Insert the stem for about half its length in a mixture of peat and sand, this time 50/50 by volume.

Rooting is slower but is usually well established by early to mid-autumn. If it has not occurred by the end of the early autumn month, leave the cuttings where they are, keep them lightly watered, and pot them in the following spring.

AFTERCARE

Potting up seedlings and rooted cuttings amounts to much the same technique, although the seedlings will tend to be more tender to handle and you should wait until they are large enough. Advice you may be given to pot them up 'when they have the first pair of true leaves' is fairly silly; many alpine cuttings are far too small at that stage.

1. Hold a leaf – *not* the main stem – and gently lever the cutting from the cuttings mixture, using a small dibber.

2. Let the root ball sit on the palm of the same hand as the one holding the leaf. Your other hand is now free to make the planting hole in the pot. Never let the stem take any strain.

3. Water the newly planted cuttings and return to the frame for growing on and hardening off.

· 8 ·
A–Z of Plants

ROCK GARDEN PLANTS

Achillea × lewisii 'King Edward'
An extremely long-flowering plant with soft yellow flowers in wide, flat heads from late spring to early autumn. Spot plant. Height 20 cm (8 in).

Aethionema 'Warley Rose'
This is in the front rank of rock garden plants. It has heads of small, rich carmine flowers and makes a neat, gnarled shrublet. 'Warley Ruber' is darker, even richer red. Spot or crevice plant. Early to mid-summer. 10 cm (4 in).

Allium oreophilum (also known as
A. ostrowskyanum)
A cheerful little ornamental onion that spreads gently by forming bulbils. Large, rounded heads of rich red, especially in the form 'Zwanenburg'. Spot plant. Early summer. 15 cm (6 in).

Alyssum saxatile 'Compactum'
One of the most popular of all rock plants. It has billowing heads of yellow flowers, known as 'gold dust', and in this compact form is highly desirable. *A.s. citrinum* is lemon yellow, but larger. Crevice. Early to mid-summer. 15 cm (6 in).

Androsace lanuginosa
Long, leafy stems arise from sparse rosettes of leaves and bear clusters of soft pink flowers on 5 cm (2 in) stems. Tolerant of winter wet, even though silky-woolly. Crevice. Mid-summer. Prostrate growing.

Aquilegia discolor
One of the smallest aquilegias, with cushions of foliage and large, blue flowers with cream centres. Delightful in a trough. Mid- to late summer. 10 cm (4 in).

Arabis blepharophylla
This plant is a cut above your average arabis. The foliage is grey-green and the conspicuous flowers are rose pink. The best forms are almost red. Small mat-former for the scree. Mid- to late spring. 8 cm (3 in).

Armeria juniperifolia (also known as
A. caespitosa)
A small, tight bun of a 'thrift' with round heads of pink flowers. Ideal for a trough, scree or crevice. 'Bevan's Variety' has deeper, rose-pink flowers. Late spring to early summer. 5 cm (2 in).

Asperula lilacaeflora caespitosa
An almost prostrate, heath-like cushion of green leaves, and masses of comparatively large, lilac-pink, stemless trumpets. Scree, trough or crevice. Early to mid-summer. 5 cm (2 in).

71

► *Linum arboreum* (yellow flowers), *Erinus alpinus* (magenta flowers) and *Arenaria purpurascens* (pink flowers) in a gravel alpine bed.

▲ Aethionema 'Warley Rose' is deservedly one of the most popular of rock plants and figures in the author's personal top ten.

► The beautifully coloured *Dianthus* 'London Brocade' is one of several garden pinks suitable for a rock garden.

Aster alpinus

The alpine aster is a neat little plant with flat rosettes of leaves and large daisies in a variety of colours. Try 'Albus' (white), 'Beechwood' (deep blue-purple), and 'Happy End' (rose pink). Spot plant, but nice in a crevice. Early summer. 15 cm (6 in).

Astilbe crispa 'Perkeo'

The best of the alpine astilbes, with feathery, crinkled leaves and also feathery heads of pink. For the shady side. Mid- to late summer. 8 cm (3 in).

Aubrieta varieties

Aubrietas are ideal crevice plants making, when cut back after flowering, neat, billowing cushions especially when allowed to grow on their sides. Try 'Blue Beauty' (compact growth, double, deep blue), 'Bressingham Pink' (double, rose pink), 'Dr. Mules' (single, deep purple), 'Mrs. Rodewald' (large, rich red flowers). There are about 50 varieties in all. Late spring to early summer. Usual spread about 30 cm (12 in).

Berberis × stenophylla 'Corallina Compacta'

A tiny, dense, evergreen bush with stiff, spiny leaves and orange flowers emerging from red buds. Spot plant. Mid-spring. 30 cm (12 in) after several years.

Campanula arvatica

A tiny, mat-forming campanula for a trough or choice spot on the scree. The flowers are like upturned, blue stars. Mid-summer. 5 cm (2 in).

Campanula carpatica

The largest campanula for rock gardens. Typically it has a mat of small, heart-shaped leaves, above which widely open cups are deep blue with a hint of purple on very short stems. One of the most effective of summer-flowering, mat-forming plants. Several varieties in shades of blue (e.g. 'Blue Clips') and white ('White Clips', 'Bressingham White'). Summer. 20 cm (8 in) or less.

Campanula cochlearifolia

The daintiest of the open-air campanulas. It has little, tubby, blue bells on fuse-wire stalks over gently wandering stems with tiny leaves. For a scree, trough or wall. Try 'Cambridge Blue' or the darker 'Miss Willmott'. A stunning hybrid, *C. × haylodgensis*, is a china-blue double, best in a crevice. Summer. 8 cm (3 in).

Celmisia coriacea

A striking, silver-foliaged plant with a rosette of upright, sword-like leaves and very large, white daisies in woolly heads. For the shady side. Summer. 30 cm (12 in).

Convolvulus cneorum

This wonderfully silver plant is only just small enough for the rock garden and should be given a well drained pocket all to itself in sun. The

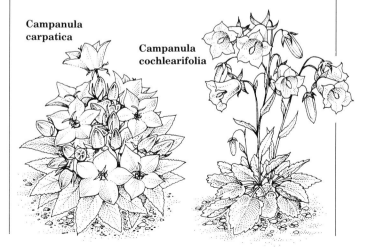

Campanula carpatica

Campanula cochlearifolia

· HANDY TIP ·

Weeding the rock garden involves a lot of kneeling. This can be uncomfortable, and kneeling pads can easily damage plants. Crouching can do long-term damage to knees. Try a halfway solution: crouch, and then kneel with one knee on the top of the opposite boot. You can weed for hours on end like this.

flowers are just like those of the hedgerow 'bindweed', but this is a shrub, and not in the least invasive. Late spring to early autumn. 15 cm (9 in) by 60 cm (24 in).

Cotoneaster congestus
This entirely prostrate shrub will grip the contours of a rock or form a neat clump up to 30 cm (12 in) high if there are no contours to follow. Blue-green foliage and red berries. Evergreen.

Crocus
There are a very large number of crocuses suitable for the rock garden, far too many to list. However, you should choose species crocus, rather than the large, Dutch kinds. The many varieties of *Crocus chrysanthus* are ideal and can be grown in groups anywhere in the rock garden. They are about 2.5 cm (1 in) high.

Cyclamen coum
This is a tiny, extremely hardy cyalamen with rounded or kidney-shaped leaves, very dark green or patterned with grey or silver. It will colonize gently by seed. The propeller-like flowers may be pink, red, deep rose-carmine or white. For the shady side. Mid-winter to early spring. A little over 5 cm (2 in).

Cyclamen hederifolium (also known as *C. neapolitanum*)
The most well known of the hardy cyclamen is very easily grown and extremely long-lived. The ivy-shaped leaves are beautifully marbled and patterned and are never the same in any two plants. The flowers are rose pink, and white ones can be obtained. For the shady side. Later summer to mid-autumn. About 8 cm (3 in).

Cytisus decumbens
A prostrate, mat-forming, deciduous shrublet with tiny leaves and bright golden flowers. Mat former. Late spring to early summer. 15 cm (6 in).

Cytisus demissus
Another deciduous, mat-forming shrub, but small enough for a trough. Small, tri-leafleted, hairy leaves and yellow flowers that are large for the size of the plant. Late spring to early summer. 8 cm (3 in).

Daphne tangutica (*Retusa* group)
These are small, almost ball-shaped, evergreen bushes with leathery, deep green leaves and terminal clusters of rose-purple flowers with a delicious scent. For a well-drained, sunny spot with a cool root run. Ideal for raised beds. Mid- to late spring. Ultimately 60 cm (24 in).

Dianthus species
This is the genus to which the pinks belong. Most garden pinks are too large for the rock garden, but there are several that are perfect rock plants and some that are small enough for a trough. Among the best are 'Little Jock', 'La Bourboule', *Dianthus myrtinervius* and *D. arvernensis*. The smallest may be planted in groups of three in gritty, sunny pockets. Summer flowering. Most are about 10 cm (4 in).

Dodecatheon 'Red Wings'
A primula relative with flowers like a cyclamen. It is one of several dodecatheons, but most of the others are too large for the rock garden. This one has 30 cm (12 in) flower stems arising from flat rosettes of leaves, and clusters of crimson flowers. For the shady side. Late spring to early summer.

Dryas octopetala
The best place for the mat of tiny, oak-like leaves of this plant is in poor soil at the edge of the rock garden. Large, white flowers are held on upright stems and turn to face the sun. *D.o.* 'Minor' is small enough for a trough. Late spring to early summer. 15 cm (6 in).

Edraianthus pumilio
This is one of the choicest little plants you can grow. It has beautiful, small tufts of short, narrow, silver leaves and almost stemless clusters of violet-blue flowers that almost hide the plant. For a scree, trough, sink or raised bed. Mid- to late summer. 5–8 cm (2–3 in).

Erinus alpinus
A tiny plant with pads of minute, toothed leaves and slightly lipped flowers in rosy mauve. It flowers very freely and seeds freely in a wall. The best forms, which come true from seed, are 'Mrs Chas Boyle' (pink), 'Dr. Hanele' (crimson), and there is a white form. Crevice. Late spring to mid-summer. 5 cm (2 in).

Erodium reichardii 'Roseum'.
You may find this labelled as *E. chamaedryoides* 'Roseum'. It is a choice alpine plant, making a small mat of neat leaves and stemless, deep rose flowers with darker veins. For a trough, sink, scree, raised bed or a gritty, sunny pocket. Early to late summer. Less than 2.5 cm (1 in).

Euryops acraeus
An intensely white-silver, domed bush with bright gold daisy flowers that stand out beautifully against the foliage. Needs a well-drained place. Spot plant. Late spring to early summer. 30 cm (12 in).

Gaultheria procumbens
An easily grown plant for peaty, lime-free conditions. It spreads by thrusting its branches shallowly underground, where they root. It has shiny, dark green leaves and white, urn-shaped flowers that are followed by bright red berries. For the shady side. Mid- to late summer. 15 cm (6 in) by about 45 cm (18 in).

Genista sagittalis
A prostrate, thornless broom with winged branches. The wings are green and narrowed at intervals. The flowers are bright yellow and borne in dense clusters. Easy in a sunny pocket. Late spring to mid-summer. 15 cm (6 in).

Gentiana acaulis
This name covers the group of spring-flowering trumpet gentians. They make small mats of leaf rosettes, from which stemless, blue trumpets of astonishing size arise. Plant them in a rich soil that is somewhat firmer than the average rock garden soil. Spring. 8 cm (3 in).

Gentiana sino-ornata
This is just one of a large group of species and hybrids that make up the Asiatic, autumn-flowering gentians. They must have a really peaty or leafy soil and it must be lime-free. Slender, sparsely-leaved stems arise from rosettes of small, narrow leaves, and produce terminal trumpets of unsurpassed loveliness in shades of blue. Try 'Devonhall', 'Midnight', and

Gentiana 'Inverleith', one of the best and most reliable of the Asiatic hybrids.

'Susan Jane'. For the shady side. Early to mid-autumn. 8 cm (3 in), spreading gently when happy.

Geranium 'Ballerina'
The hardy cranesbills, not to be confused with greenhouse 'geraniums', which belong to the genus *Pelargonium*, include quite a few lovely rock plants, among which is 'Ballerina', a hybrid with rounded flowers of lilac-pink heavily veined in deepest purple. Spot plant. Summer. 15 cm (6 in).

Gypsophila repens
Like a miniature version of the border gypsophilas, with branched stems flying off in all directions and making clouds of little white or pink flowers. Try 'Dorothy Teacher' (long flowering) and 'Rosea' (a good pink). Early summer to early autumn. 10 cm (4 in).

Haberlea rhodopensis
A leafy plant, making rosettes of leathery, bright olive-green, toothed leaves. The flowers are pale lilac, somewhat primula-like, and gold in the throat. 'Virginale' is white. For a crevice on the shady side, where it can be grown on its side. Mid-spring to early summer. 23 cm (9 in).

Hebe 'Carl Teschner'
A fairly stiff, procumbent plant with dark green leaves on blue-black stems and freely produced spikes of violet-blue flowers with white throats. Early to mid-summer. 20 cm (18 in).

77

Helianthemum varieties

Helianthemums are the rock roses that make such attractive pools of bright colour in the summer rock garden. They delight in a sunny position and a poorish soil and are mainly prostrate shrubs. Cut them back after flowering and they will flower again. There are many varieties, among which are the excellent 'Bens', called after Scottish mountains. Colours range through reds, orange, yellow and white and there are doubles and singles. Mat formers. All summer. Around 20 cm (8 in) by about 60 cm (24 in).

Helichrysum milfordiae

This intensely silver-woolly, cushion-forming plant is not very easy but is one to try at all costs. Flower buds just like old-fashioned pink-and-white striped humbug sweets sit stemless and open in sunny weather to white, red-backed, everlasting flowers. Grow in a trough or raised bed, preferably in contact with rock, and cover with a sheet of glass in winter. A long period in summer. 5 cm (2 in).

Hepatica nobilis

An anemone-like, graceful plant with kidney-shaped leaves and round, six to nine-petalled flowers, usually in blue, but sometimes pink. *H.* × *media* 'Ballardii' is one of the best of all rock garden plants and has larger, perfectly round flowers in clear blue. For the shady side. Mid- to late spring. Around 20 cm (8 in).

Hypericum olympicum

A mass of upright stems fan out from a woody base, and each bears one or more very large, rich yellow flowers with prominent yellow stamens. The buds are spirally veined in orange-pink. *H.o.* 'Citrinum' is a lovely, lemon yellow. Spot plant. Late spring to mid summer. 25 cm (10 in).

Iberis 'Little Gem'

A dwarf, shrubby plant with flat heads of white flowers. Easy to grow in a pocket in full sun. Mat forming. Late spring. About 10 cm (4 in) and a little wider.

Iris chamaeiris

A small iris with stiffly upright leaves and very large flowers for its size in shades of white, yellow, blue or purple. 'Jackanapes' and 'Campbellii' are the best known forms. Plant in a group as spot plants. Mid- to late spring. 13–25 cm (5–10 in).

Iris pumila

This is often confused with the above plant, but is significantly smaller. It is, in effect, a miniature flag iris with flowers that are almost stemless, making them seem very large. The range of colours is similar to *I. chamaeiris*. Spot plant, but plant in a group. Mid-spring. 10 cm (4 in).

Kalmiopsis leachiana

This is one of the most beautiful of all alpine shrubs, growing to be a dwarf, rounded, evergreen bush with flowers like wide open bells. They are rich pink and large for the size of the shrub. The named varieties 'Le Piniec', 'Glendoick' and 'Umpqua Valley' are the ones to choose from. For a gritty but peaty, lime-free soil on the shady side.

Leontopodium alpinum

The alpine edelweiss is mentioned here only because it is so famous a plant. Otherwise it is not worth growing. Its flannel-like flower heads, white at first, become dingy and unattractive.

Leucogynes grandiceps

A lovely plant, known as the New Zealand edelweiss. It has dense, intensely silvered foliage, which is its main attraction. The flower clusters at the ends of the branches are yellow. It needs a gritty but leafy or peaty soil and shade in the hottest part of the day. Summer. Grows to 15 cm (6 in).

Lewisia varieties
There are many lewisias, but the ones to try are the ones listed in catalogues just as *Lewisia* varieties or sometimes *L. cotyledon* varieties. These have rosettes of leathery, succulent leaves, from which arise branched stems bearing quite large, starry flowers in brilliant colours (red, orange, yellow or white). They must be grown on their sides in a wall or rock crevice. Late spring to early summer. 30 cm (12 in).

Linum 'Gemmell's Hybrid'
One of the longest-flowering of rock plants, lasting all summer. It is a compact, shrubby plant with dark green, glossy leaves and large, glossily golden flowers. Spot plant. 20 cm (8 in).

Lithodora diffusa
This ever-popular plant, usually found as one of the varieties 'Heavenly Blue' or 'Grace Ward', is not as easy as people often think, although given the right conditions of a lime-free soil and full sun it will thrive beautifully, making a wide mat of dark green foliage and flowering for a long period. The flowers are gentian blue. Mat-former. Summer. 10 cm (4 in) by about 20 cm (24 in).

Mentha requinii
A delightful, tiny, closely mat-forming plant with minute leaves and clusters of very small, lilac flowers held tightly above the leaves. The foliage is strongly aromatic, smelling refreshingly of peppermint. For the shady side, but in a gritty soil. Early to mid-summer. No height at all.

Moltkia × intermedia
A shrubby plant, and one that loves limestone. It has greyish, hairy leaves and spreading croziers of bright blue, tubular to funnel-shaped flowers. Spot plant in a sunny position. Early summer. 25 cm (10 in).

Morisia monanthos
The contrast between the dark green cushions of leaf rosettes and the stemless, rich yellow flowers is dramatic in such a small plant. It is long flowering and perfect in a trough or scree but needs a poor soil to keep it in character. Mid-spring to mid-summer. 5 cm (2 in).

Narcissus
The dwarf daffodils and narcissi are ideal for the rock garden in early and mid-spring. There are many different kinds, and many varieties of each kind. Generally speaking, a height of 20 cm (8 in) is the maximum for an average rock garden.

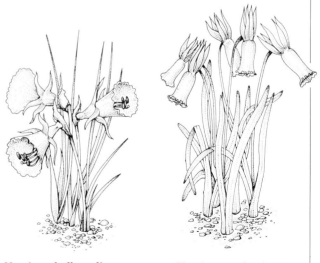

Narcissus bulbocodium   **Narcissus cyclamineus**

◄ One of the many helianthemums that provide weeks of colour in summer and early autumn.

► *Penstemon fruticosus scouleri* – a dwarf shrub from America.

This colourful and varied
planting includes sedums,
primulas and a dianthus.

Origanum laevigatum

A robust, but quite small and unusual marjoram. It makes neat mats of small, dark green leaves, from which long, wiry stems arise and arch over, bearing branched sprays of small, reddish purple flowers. A most elegant spot plant. Late summer to mid-autumn. The stems are 25 cm (10 in) long but arch, making the height of the plant in flower not more than 15 cm (6 in).

Ourisia caespitosa gracilis

This is one of the choicest little plants for the shady part of the rock garden. It makes a tight mat of grey-green, notched leaves, and has slender, wiry stems with clusters of white flowers. Late spring to early summer. 10 cm (4 in).

Oxalis adenophylla

A neat clump of bulbs, heavily coated in fibre. The grey-green leaves are made up of a dozen or so folded leaflets like ruffs or half-open parasols. Round and silky pink flowers, paler at the centres. Spot plant. Mid- to late spring 10 cm (4 in).

Papaver alpinum

These little alpine poppies have finely lined, grey-green foliage, slender flower stems, and cup-shaped flowers in pink, white, orange and yellow. Spot plants. All summer. 15 cm (6 in).

Penstemon davidsonii

One of several small, shrubby penstemons, entirely different from their border cousins. This is a typical, contour-hugging, dwarf, gnarled shrub with surprisingly large, tubular-lipped flowers in clusters. The species varies from lavender pink to ruby red, and although the naming in the others is muddled it doesn't matter, as they are all good. Spot plants. Mid- to late summer. All are under 30 cm (12 in).

Penstemon pinifolius

Mentioned because it is so unlike the others. It has softer, more slender stems, leaves like tiny pine needles, and long, thin flowers of brilliant scarlet. Late summer. 20 cm (8 in).

Phlox douglasii

A very neat phlox, making tight, prickly mats and with rounded, mauve flowers. There are many varieties, such as 'Apple Blossom' (lilac pink), 'Apollo' (rich violet), 'Boothman's Variety' (large, circular flowers, clear mauve with darker centres), 'Iceberg' (compact, white), and 'Crackerjack' (compact, brilliant crimson). Excellent, neat mat formers for scree, crevices, raised beds, and walls. Late spring. 5–10 cm (2–4 in): spreads from 15 cm (6 in) to 30 cm (12 in).

Phlox subulata

This is a coarser, larger species, appearing in gardens only as its highly colourful and valuable varieties. There are about 40 available. Among some of the best are 'G.F. Wilson' (clear blue), 'Sampson' (deep rose), 'Scarlet Flame' (carmine-scarlet) and 'Temiskaming', which is the most vigorous and is magenta – not everyone's colour. Mat formers. Mid- to late spring. On average 15 cm (6 in) with a spread of 75 cm (30 in).

Phyllodoce × intermedia

A dwarf, heather-like shrub for a peaty, lime-free spot. It has heather-like foliage and masses of urn-shaped flowers, which are crimson purple in 'Drummondii', lighter coloured in 'Fred Stoker'. For the shady side. Late spring. 25 cm (10 in).

Physoplexis comosa (also known as *Phyteuma comosum*)

Often thought to be difficult, this highly unusual plant, whose flower heads look like a collection of tiny, blue soda bottles, is easy enough in a crevice, but it is worth taking precautions against slugs. It is related to campanulas. Summer. 8 cm (3 in).

Potentilla eriocarpa
A shrubby plant, easy to grow, with woody stems in spreading mats. The foliage is deeply lobed and grey-green. The flowers are pure, light yellow. Mat former. Early summer to early autumn. 5 cm (2 in).

Potentilla nitida
This most choice plant makes pads of silky, three-lobed leaves and bears stemless flowers like small, single roses. Generally pink, but try 'Rubra', whose flowers are rich, deep rose. For a crevice, scree, trough or raised bed. Summer. Less than 2.5 cm (1 in).

Primula × pubsecens varieties
There are so many excellent primulas for the rock garden that it is possible only to give you one or two examples of the best groups. This group belongs to the European primulas and consists of colour variants of a hybrid between two species from the Alps. They are easy to grow and love a crevice. Among the best are 'Bewerley White', 'Boothman's Variety' (bright crimson), 'Mrs J.H. Wilson' (deep violet) and 'Rufus' (brick red). Crevice or gritty pocket. Mid- to late spring. 10–15 cm (4–6 in).

Primula warshenewskyana
This is a tiny Asiatic primula which, unusually, spreads gently by runners. Its little, rose pink flowers are stemless and the plant is ideal for a choice spot on the shady side or in a partly shaded trough that does not become dry. Early to mid-spring. Less than 2.5 cm (1 in).

Primula denticulata
The 'drumstick' primula is one of the very large number of Asiatic primulas available to gardeners, most of which are too large for the average rock garden. This one is good on the shady side and looks 'right' near water, if you have it. The flower heads are as round as golf balls and about the same size. Early to late spring. 25 cm (10 in).

Pulsatilla vulgaris
There are varieties of this alpine anemone in anything from lilac to clear, light red. Several stems arise from finely cut foliage, each carrying a very large, chalice-shaped flower. Spot plant. Mid- to late spring. 25 cm (10 in).

Ramonda myconi
A plant making large rosettes, up to 25 cm (10 in) across, of rough leaves with coppery hairs beneath. The flowers are flat, five-petalled and rich mauve with a central pyramid of yellow stamens. It should be grown in shade, in a crevice

Ramonda myconi

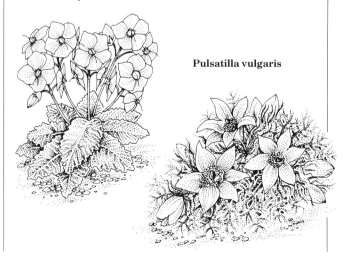

Pulsatilla vulgaris

Sempervivums and other
plants on an expertly built
rock garden.

Sedum spathulifolium **'Cape Blanco'. This plant comes from the Cape Blanco State Park, Oregon, where the Siskyou National Forest meets the sea. It is often wrongly labelled 'Cappa Blanca'.**

or wall, and on its side. Once established it will remain for several years and even stand up to drought, curling up but quickly recovering when watered. Mid- to late spring. 15 cm (6 in).

Ranunculus gramineus

A grassy buttercup with erect, almost iris-like leaves and bright yellow flowers. It is small when young but taller when older, and the best place for it is the scree. Summer. 15–25 cm (6–10 in).

Raoulia australis

Makes a film of tiny, silvery-hairy leaves that develops patches of yellow when it flowers. For a sunny, finely-textured scree. All summer. No height at all.

Raoulia hookeri

This species is larger and intensely silver, making higher attractive mats of small rosettes. It is ideal for the scree but comes into its own in a trough or on a raised bed. It rarely flowers, but somehow the fluffy, yellow flower heads would spoil it anyway. Less than 2.5 cm (1 in).

Rhododendron

The rhododendrons for the rock garden should be truly dwarf, which means that an ultimate height of 60 cm (24 in) is too much for the average rock garden but just right for larger ones. They should be grown on the shady side and should be given as leafy or peaty a soil as possible, as they have fine, fibrous root systems and hate lime. They are mostly spring flowering, but a colour sequence is possible over several weeks. Some examples of true dwarf rhododendrons:

R. campylogynum 'Salmon Pink'. Small, thimble-like flowers. Mid-spring. 30 cm (1 ft).

R.c. myrtilloides. Pink. Only 15 cm (6 in).

'Chikor'. Bright yellow. Late spring. Less than 30 cm (12 in).

R. hanceanum 'Nanum'. Completely covers itself with bright, creamy yellow flowers. Late spring to early summer. About 30 cm (12 in).

R. pemakoense. Large, pale pink flowers hiding the 30 cm (12 in) shrub. Early to mid-spring (too early for cold areas, where the flowers may be frosted).

'Egret'. Dainty white bells, almost like a large-flowered heather. Late spring. About 30 cm (12 in)

Saxifraga

A very large genus of plants. As you progress with your rock gardening, you may well find them so interesting that you venture into some of the byways of saxifrages, but there are two main groups that form part of the backbone of any good rock garden: the cushion and the silver saxifrages.

● *Cushion saxifrages* generally make little domes or domed mats of closely-packed, needle-like foliage and are rather like hedgehogs. Their flowers sit on them singly with almost no stems or rise above the cushions with several to a stem.

Saxifraga × apiculata is the most robust of all, making wide, undulating, cushiony, prickly mats. The primrose-yellow flowers are in sprays. It will take full sun all day except in the warmest places, but most of this section need shade at the hottest part of the day.

S. burseriana is typical of the kind that have stemless flowers close to the cushion. Its varieties

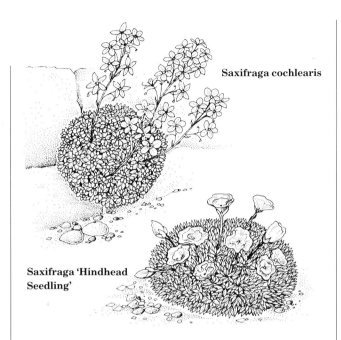

Saxifraga cochlearis

Saxifraga 'Hindhead Seedling'

– 'Brookside' (large, white flowers), 'His Majesty' (large, pink tinted) and 'Sulphurea' (soft yellow) – are among the best of all cushion saxifrages.

'Cranbourne' is the best deep pink of the cushion forms.

'Faldonside' is unsurpassed as a stemless yellow.

● *Silver saxifrages* make cushions or clumps of stiff, more-or-less flat rosettes, in which the leaves are to varying degrees encrusted with silvery lime deposits. The flowers are in generous sprays, on much taller stems than the cushion saxifrages. They are usually white, but many have pink or red spots. Silver saxifrages are happy in sun or a little shade and are ideal crevice and wall plants.

S. callosa is typical and has blue-green, heavily limy leaves 5 cm (2 in) long. The arching stems carry many-flowered sprays of white. Early to mid-summer. 30 cm (12 in).

S. cochlearis is smaller and more clump-forming and the leaves are spoon-shaped. The flowers are white and on 20 cm (8 in) stems. *S.c.* 'Major' is larger in every way, and *S.c.* 'Minor' is very much smaller, making a rounded, neat cushion suitable for a trough.

S. cotyledon is unusual in disliking lime in the soil. It is dramatic in a crevice, especially in the form 'Southside Seedling' whose flowers, in sprays 60 cm (24 in) long or more, arch over from a vertical crevice in a shower of white, heavily speckled with rose red.

Sedum spathulifolium
There are many sedums suitable for the rock garden, but this is probably the best of them. It makes neat mounds of soft, fleshy leaves on short, brittle, waxy stems. The whole plant is covered with a white, powdery bloom, which is most marked in the smaller form 'Cape Blanco', turning the whole plant white. 'Purpureum' has purple leaves with a bloomy finish. The flowers are yellow and borne in a handsome head. For a wall, raised bed or scree. Summer. 13 cm (5 in).

Sempervivum
The plants known as 'house leeks' come in a great variety of sizes, but always consist of rosettes of succulent, pointed leaves. Sometimes in the larger species – they are flat; in others they are tightly balled and may even be covered with a fine network like spiders' webs. They are extremely easy to grow, prefer full sun and a poorish soil, wall or crevice, and one or two are small enough for a trough. Their flowers are not very pretty.

Silene schafta
A plant valuable for its late flowering, but not very easy to place because of its magenta colouring. Mat former. Mid-summer to mid-autumn. 15 cm (6 in) by about 30 cm (12 in).

Sisyrinchium angustifolium
This is one of a group of small plants with iris-like foliage and attractive, starry flowers. In this species they are clear blue and it is a most desirable plant. The yellow *S. brachypus* should be avoided, as it is very invasive by means of seed. Spot plant. Mid-summer to early autumn. 20 cm (8 in).

Thymus serpyllum
The European wild thyme is a mat-forming plant with minute leaves and small heads of flowers anywhere from light pink to purple and crimson. There are many garden forms. For scree, a gritty pocket or a wall. Mid-spring to mid-summer. About 2.5 cm (1 in).

Viola calcarata
A miniature, long-spurred pansy. It is a small, compact grower with flowers in many colours from light blue to deep purple and yellow. It and several other alpine violas make ideal, small spot plants in rock garden pockets. Much of summer. 10 cm (4 in).

Vitaliana primuliflora (also known as *Douglasia vitaliana*).
Almost directly on the silvery-green cushion of needle-like foliage are yellow flowers just like half-open primroses. It is a perfect subject for a trough, raised bed, or especially a crevice or a wall. Mid- to late spring. 5 cm (2 in).

Sempervivum species

CONIFERS FOR ROCK GARDENS

Conifers in troughs and sinks will be much smaller than those in the open ground, but you should still obtain the true dwarf varieties.

Abies balsmaea 'Hudsonia'

A truly dwarf form of the silver fir. It forms a flat-topped, dense, compact bush which, after 30 years is likely to be only 75 cm × 1.2 m (30 in by 4 ft).

Cedrus libani

The Lebanon cedar has produced several dwarf forms, all of which are small enough for the average-sized rock garden. 'Nana' is very slow growing, dense and conical; 'Sargentii' is not quite as dwarf, but elegantly weeping.

Chamaecyparis lawsoniana

There are more dwarf forms of Lawson's cypress than of any other conifer, but you may find varieties on sale that eventually become quite large. The following are reliable:

'Aurea Densa'. This is compact and conical, reaching 2 m (6½ ft) only after many years. The foliage is golden yellow and in flattened sprays.

'Forsteckensis' has a dense, globular habit, so dense as to appear almost mossy. After 30 years it will attain a size of about 90 cm × 1.2 m (3 × 4 ft).

'Minima Glauca' is another globular conifer, with foliage in flat, deep green sprays. It is rather larger than the aforementioned.

Chamaecyparis obtusa

This has more really tiny varieties than any other conifer. The following are ideal:

'Nana' (not to be confused with the much larger 'Nana Gracilis') is made up of neat, twisted sprays of almost black green. After 30 years it will only be 60 × 75 cm (24 × 30 in).

'Nana Aurea' is slightly looser than the above and probably the best dwarf golden conifer for the rock garden.

'Tempelhof' is a dense, deep green, dwarf bush, considerably larger than 'Nana', but perfect for the rock garden.

Cryptomeria japonica

A tall tree, but one of its dwarfest forms, 'Vilmoriniana', is ideal for a trough or raised bed. It makes a perfect, bronzed globe, only 20 × 30 cm (8 × 12 in) after 12–15 years.

Juniperus communis

This is best known for the ultimate dwarf conifer, J.c. 'Compressa', otherwise known as the Noah's Ark Juniper, which makes a perfect, pointed, cylindrical column of needle-like leaves and never reaches more than 90 cm (36 in) in its entire existence. Perfect for a trough.

Juniperus horizontalis 'Bar Harbour'

A perfectly prostrate, blue, carpet-forming conifer, exactly right for the edges of the rock garden where it merges with other features.

Picea abies

The Norway spruce has some delightful dwarf forms: 'Clanbrassiliana' is dwarf, making a dome about 1.2 × 2.4 m (4 ft × 8 ft) after 30 years and suitable for the edge of a moderately sized rock garden.

'Nidiformis' is a rock garden favourite, making a nest-shaped bush only 60 cm × 1.8 m (2 × 6 ft) after 30 years.

Picea glauca 'Albertiana Conica'
One of the most widely sold conifers for the rock garden. It may become large in time, but after 15 years will still only be a perfect cone, 90 cm (36 in) high and 75 cm (30 in) across at the base.

The intriguing shapes of dwarf conifers are as architecturally important to the rock garden as forest trees are to a general landscape.

Thuja orientalis 'Rosedalis'
A soft, fluffily foliaged conifer with subtle colourings in green and russet. It will attain a height of only 90 cm (36 in) after 25 years but will also be 90 cm (36 in) wide.

WATER PLANTS FOR ROCK GARDEN POOLS

Nymphaea

Water-lilies suitable for rock garden pools may be small (spread 0.3 sq m/3 sq ft), medium (0.6 to 1.3 sq m/ 6 to 15 sq ft), or large (1.3 to 1.8 sq m / 15 to 20 sq ft). The large ones are only appropriate for larger pools. Planting depths are approximately: small (S) 38 cm (15 in), medium (M) 50 cm (20 in), and large (L) 60 cm (24 in).

● *Red water-lilies*
'Attraction' (M). A free-flowering plant. The carmine flowers have white tips.

'Escarboucle' (M). Perhaps the best known. The large, vivid vermillion flowers are long lasting.

Fig. 23 Blocks may be required to lift young non-oxygenating plants to the water surface.

(a) At planting

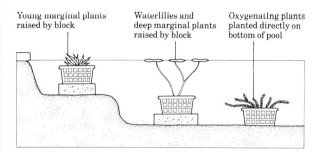

(b) When established

'Froebelii' (S). Dark red flowers and deep green foliage. Scented.

'James Brydon' (M). Semi-double, crimson flowers and deservedly one of the most popular of all.

'Rene Gerrard' (M). The colour is rich, deep pink.

● *Pink water-lilies*
'Amabilis' (M). A lovely plant, whose flowers shade from deep rose to light salmon pink on foliage that starts off purple and gradually becomes green.

'Marliacea Carnea' (L). Very light pink, deepening towards the centre. A lovely water-lily, but only for larger pools.

'Madame Wilfron Gonnère' (M). A truly double water-lily in white, flushed with rose pink.

'Mrs Richmond' (M). Unusually large flowers, light pink at first, deepening later to rose pink.

'Peter Slocum' (M). A new water-lily from America with double, soft pink flowers that are sweetly fragrant.

'Rose Arey' (S). Bright cerise, fragrant flowers with petals that uncurve, making a most attractive round bloom. The stamens are orange and the foliage is purple at first, becoming green.

● *Yellow water-lilies*
'Marliacea Chromatella' (M). Perhaps the most popular water-lily of all. It has large, broadly starry flowers in a fine shade of soft but strong yellow. It is free flowering and easy.

'Moorei' (M) is not unlike the above but the flower is slightly less open.

× *helvola* (S) is a very small water-lily that can be grown in the smallest pool. It has starry, canary-yellow flowers through a long season. The foliage is naturally strongly mottled.

'Sunrise' (M) and *odorata* 'Sulphurea' (M) are fine yellow water-lilies, but are not to be attempted in colder areas. They have a strong tropical element in their make-up and, while hardy enough, will not flower unless the summers are fairly hot.

● *White water-lilies*
'Albatros' (M) has large, white, star-shaped flowers and foliage that is purple at first, turning green.

'Carolinea Nivea' (S), although a small plant, has large flowers. They are beautifully scented.

'Gonnère' (S) is a little larger, but has even larger flowers, which are snow white and double.

'Marliacea Albida' (M) is an easily grown variety and, although classed here as medium, is only for larger pools. The large, white flowers are fragrant.

Oxygenating plants

Callitriche autumnalis One of the few oxygenators that remains active during winter.

Callitriche verna The water starwort makes tufts of thready, underwater foliage and rises to the surface in summer. Good protection for fish.

Elodea canadensis Canadian pond weed is a first-class oxygenator, but it builds up rapidly and you will need to pull some out from time to time.

Hottonia palustris The water violet is unusual among oxygenators because it flowers, with sprays of small, lavender blooms up to 15 cm (6 in) above water level.

Myriophyllum verticillatum has long, slender stems set with whorls of radiating, much-divided foliage.

Ranunculus aquatilis Another flowering oxygenator with pure white blooms 2.5 cm (1 in) above water level. The submerged foliage is thread-like, while surface leaves are three-lobed.

Marginal plants
The following are in keeping with an adjacent rock garden:

Anopogeton distachyum is a deep marginal, to be planted as if it were a water-lily. It has strap-shaped, floating leaves and heads of lovely white flowers. Water hawthorn. About 10 cm (4 in).

Caltha palustris The marsh marigold or kingcup has lush, dark green foliage and large, brilliant

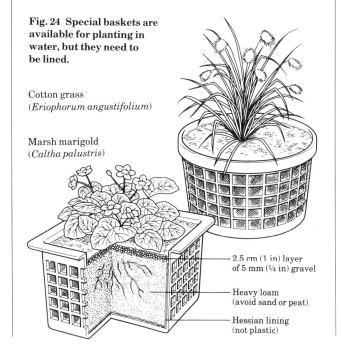

Fig. 24 Special baskets are available for planting in water, but they need to be lined.

Cotton grass (*Eriophorum angustifolium*)

Marsh marigold (*Caltha palustris*)

2.5 cm (1 in) layer of 5 mm (¼ in) gravel

Heavy loam (avoid sand or peat)

Hessian lining (not plastic)

◄ A perfect example of rock-garden building, in which water, rocks and plants have been brought together in delightful harmony.

► The double marsh marigold, *Caltha palustris* 'Flore Pleno', is not an alpine, but a marginal plant that associates perfectly with the plants of the rock garden.

golden-yellow flowers in early spring and summer. 30 cm (1 ft). *C.p.* 'Alba' is white. The double form, *C.p.* 'Flore Pleno' is a smaller cultivar. It has golden-yellow blooms like miniature pompon chrysanthemums and neat mounds of foliage.

Carex stricta 'Bowles' Golden' Not strictly a grass, but with the appearance of one with stiffly arched, golden leaves. 35 cm (14 in).

Eriophorum angustifolium The cotton grass makes neat tufts of rush-like foliage and has slender stems with round heads of white cotton wool. 30 cm (12 in).

Myosotis palustris The water forget-me-not is the perfect marginal for association with a rock garden with pale blue, yellow-eyed flowers from mid-spring to mid-summer. 20 cm (8 in).

Appendix

SOCIETIES

The Alpine Garden Society
AGS Centre
Avon Bank
Pershore
Worcestershire WR10 3JP
England

Groups in Australia, New Zealand, Canada, etc. For information contact the above. Publishes quarterly bulletin, annual seed list. Comprehensive book list. Several annual shows in UK and Ireland. Local groups meet, usually monthly.

The Scottish Rock Garden Club
Membership Secretary:
Mrs J. Thomlinson
1 Hillcrest Road
Bearsden
Glasgow G61 2EB
Scotland

Publishes *The Rock Garden* twice yearly. Annual seed list of over 4000 species. Twice yearly book list. Several shows. Regional groups.

The American Rock Garden Society
Jacques Mommens
P.O. Box 67
Millwood
New York 10546
USA

Membership benefits include the quarterly bulletin and a seed exchange.

MAIL-ORDER SUPPLIERS, UK

Holden Clough Nursery
Bolton by Bowland
Clitheroe
Lancashire

Inshriach Alpine Plant Nursery
(Jack Drake)
Aviemore
Inverness-shire
Scotland

Greenslacks Nurseries
Ocot Lane
Scammonden
Huddersfield
Yorkshire

W.E.Th. Ingwersen Ltd
Gravetye Nursery
East Grinstead
Sussex

Hartside Nursery Garden
Nr. Alston
Cumbria

Lingen Alpine Nursery
Lingen, nr. Bucknell
Shropshire

Potterton and Martin
The Cottage Nursery
Moortown Road
Nettleton
Nr. Caistor
North Lincolnshire

Stapeley Water Gardens
Nantwich
Cheshire

MAIL-ORDER SUPPLIERS, USA

Daystar
R.F.D.2
Litchfield
Maine 04350

Lilypons Water Gardens
6800 Lilypons Road
P.O. Box 10
Lilypons
Maryland 21717

Maver Rare Plant Nursery
P.O. Box 18754
Seattle
Washington 98118

Rakestraw's Perennials Garden
3094 South Term Street
Burton
Michigan 48529

Rice Creek Gardens
1315 66th Avenue N.E.
Minneapoliss
Minnesota 55432

Rocknoll Nursery
9210 U.S. 50
Hillsboro
Ohio 45133

Siskiyou Rare Plant Nursery
2825 Cummings Road
Medford
Oregon 97501

Index

Page numbers in *italics* indicate an illustration or boxed table.
See also A–Z of Plants, 71–93.